I Will Survive In Jesus' Name!

Jennifer Mitchell Earley

APHESIS PUBLISHING COMPANY

Unless otherwise identified, Scripture taken from HOLY BIBLE, NEW INTERNATIONAL VERSION®. Copyright © 1973, 1978, 1984 by International Bible Society. Used by permission of Zondervan Publishing House. All rights reserved.

The "NIV" and "New International Version" trademarks are registered in the United States Patent and Trademark Office by International Bible Society. Use of either trademark requires the permission of International Bible Society.

"Scripture quotations taken from AMPLIFIED BIBLE, Copyright © 1954, 1958, 1962, 1964, 1965, 1987 by the Lockman Foundation. All rights reserved. Used by permission. (www.lockman.org)"

Scripture quotations marked (NLT) are from the Holy Bible: New Living Translation Version of the Bible. Emphasis within Scripture quotes is the author's own.

ISBN 0-9772056-0-6
LCCN 2005907332

PUBLISHER'S NOTE
Names, characters, places, and incidents either are products of the author's imagination or are used fictitiously, and any resemblance to actual persons, living or dead, business establishments, events or locales, is entirely coincidental.

ATTENTION CHURCHES, UNIVERSITIES, COLLEGES, AND PROFESSIONAL ORGANIZATIONS: Quantity discounts are available on bulk purchases of this book for educational, gift purposes, or as premiums for increasing magazine subscriptions or renewals. Special books or book excerpts can also be created to fit specific needs. For information, please contact Aphesis Publishing Company, P.O. Box 221366, Beachwood, OH 44122; JimMitchell@aphesispublishing.com, ph 216-253-2531.

Cover by Ill for Unigraphics 216.587.0077

DEDICATION

*T*hank you, Lord, for trusting and imparting to me your vision, purpose, and gifting. Bless your name, Lord, for your Word says that you equip the called, and you definitely equipped me for this! Thank you, mom and dad, for your never ending support. I pray daily that God will bless you for the many selfless sacrifices that you have made for Jeff and me throughout the years. To the Maryland Mitchell's, I love you guys! Danielle and Michael, thank you for being my "eyes." To my MBNA colleagues and college crew, you will never know how God has used and continues to use you to bless me. Thank you for reminding me of the power of laughter. To Charles and Alicia, thank you for countless visits to Applebee's and for showing me a godly marriage, which makes me want to try it again. To the Booker family – thank you for "much prayer", late night conversations, and good coffee! Kathy, you're definitely my "iron!" To Pastors Scott and Tyear McCrary and my Ecclesia Fellowship Family, thank you for your guidance, encouragement, and support.

TABLE OF CONTENTS

PART I - HOW DID I GET HERE?

PART II – STANDING ON GOD'S WORD

PART III – FINDING THE COURAGE TO LEAVE

PART IV – LEARNING TO FORGIVE

PART V – THE PATH TO PEACE

PREFACE

Millions of Christians, from all walks of life and denominations, have either known someone who has been faced with domestic violence or have dealt with issues of domestic violence themselves. While all communities of faith are plagued by domestic violence, there are certain issues that arise for Christians because our lives are governed by the Word of God.

Scriptures from both the Old and New Testaments of the Bible speak to the roles of men and women in relationships, the structure of family, Jesus' suffering and sacrifice, compassion, and forgiveness. These scriptures are most commonly misused and misinterpreted to justify why women should remain in a relationship despite being abused as well as when trying to answer questions about deservedness, cause of abuse, and in deciding whether to forgive the abusive partners.

Abuse is a pattern of hurtful behavior that one partner in an intimate relationship uses to control the other. A common myth is that abuse is the result of one person becoming angry and "losing control". On the contrary, abuse is actually a way that a person attempts to gain control over his intimate partner. When abuse has occurred once in a relationship, it is likely to happen again.

Abuse takes on many forms:

PHYSICAL ABUSE – BEHAVIOR THAT INFLICTS HARM ON A PERSON

- punching
- slapping
- kicking
- shoving
- hair pulling
- choking
- striking with an object
- physical confinement
- isolation
- grabbing
- biting
- throwing objects
- scratching
- burning

SEXUAL ABUSE – SEXUAL ADVANCES THAT ARE UNWANTED OR MAKE A PERSON FEEL UNCOMFORTABLE

- unwanted touching
- sexual relations without consent
- humiliating or painful acts
- being called sexual names
- threatening to get another sex partner
- accusations of sleeping around
- striking with an object
- making fun of sexual ability

PHYSIOLOGICAL/EMOTIONAL – BEHAVIOR INTENDED TO CAUSE EMOTIONAL AND PSYCHOLOGICAL DISTRESS

- acts intended to humiliate, control or intimidate
- stalking or following
- extreme expressions of jealousy
- threatening the partner or people related to them
- intimidation
- put-downs
- telling a person's secrets
- possessiveness
- isolating a person from one's family and friends
- destroying gifts, cards or letters
- damaging a car, home or other prized possessions
- being blamed for a partner's own faults
- emotional withholding
- economic control

VERBAL ABUSE – BEHAVIOR THAT CAUSES HARM WITH WORDS

- name-calling
- ridiculing
- degrading
- saying "nobody will ever be with you"
- insults
- public humiliation
- yelling

Domestic violence is a serious criminal offense that results in physical, emotional and financial harm. It is also very detrimental to the victims' faith because it attacks the very source of their strength by destroying their hope for safe, peaceful lives for themselves and their children.

It is my hope that this book will help you heal from the sense of betrayal, emotional pain, and spiritual damage created by and resulting from abuse. Please remember that no one has the right to hurt you. Domestic violence is a crime and is contrary to God's Word.

Part I

How did I get here?

Lean on, trust in, and be confident in the Lord with all your heart and mind and do not rely on your own insight or understanding. In all your ways know, recognize, and acknowledge Him and He will direct and make straight and plain your paths.

Proverbs 3:5-6 (AMP)

CHAPTER ONE

OVERLOOKING THE OBVIOUS

So much has happened - too much, too fast, too rocky. Somewhere along the line, I lost focus. I lost track of God, she thought...

═══════════════

Kim rededicated her life to Christ about three years ago and had been sold out for Jesus every since. She had quit her job as a Speech and Language Pathologist and decided to go back to school to work on her Ph.D. in Urban Education. As an elected official, Kim was the youngest school board member ever to be elected in her community. She had a passion for education and the study of child development.

She was young and full of life and energy. The

only thing missing was companionship. Yes, she had her girls and she was very close to her parents, but Kim desperately wanted someone to share her life with. In her spare time she read every book written by T.D. Jakes that she could put her hands on. Kim was definitely serious about her relationship with God. A true party girl, Kim severed all "worldly" ties. She no longer went out to clubs, smoked cigarettes, nor drank alcohol.

Kim was truly on fire for the Lord. Instead of trying to keep up with every social event in the city, Kim was trying to attend every church service, revival, and explosion that she could find.

Kim always found it therapeutic to write her feelings down. The problem is that she was never very consistent in keeping up with her journal. She was notorious for having several half-written journals tossed here and there around her house.

Kim began journaling again when she met Conrad. Journaling helped Kim to sort out her feelings. Things didn't seem quite so overwhelming when she wrote them down on paper.

It was a beautiful fall day. The leaves had turned a bright red-orange and brown. It was the end of fall and most of the trees were bare. Kim watched absent-mindly as the last couple of leaves fell off the tree in her front yard. Pretty soon it will be winter and snow will cover the ground instead of leaves.

Kim made herself a hot cup of coffee and curled up on her living room couch. She was very tired, because she had not been able to sleep for the last couple of nights.

Time had really gotten away from her. She continued to stare out of her living room window watching the leaves fall as she had for the last hour. Kim had a lot on her mind and she was trying to gather her thoughts in order to make some sense out of her life. Her head was pounding despite the fact that she had taken two aspirin about an hour ago.

Out of the corner of her eye she caught a glimpse of her journal buried under a pile of old newspapers and bills. Kim mustered up the energy to get up from the couch to retrieve her journal. She rummaged through her bag to find an ink pen. She exhaled as she began writing. She didn't even realize that she had been holding her breath as her thoughts flowed on to the page.

My relationship with Conrad, let's see...In the beginning it was wonderful! I will admit that I was very apprehensive about the difference in our ages (I, was 33 and he, was 26 – turning 27 on that Sunday). Initially, I wasn't going to talk to him, but he called me the next day and really impressed me with his conversation. He addressed my anxieties regarding our age difference at the onset of the conversation. I was definitely WOWED! She wrote. Kim smiled as she recalled the conversation, *I had never met a man, my age or older, and DEFINITELY NOT HIS AGE, who confronted a problem head on.*

I met Conrad when I went bowling at the neighborhood bowling alley with Lydia. Instantly, I was intrigued by him. When I got home that evening, I prayed that God would take him away. I knew that my heart was in danger of being captured. Of course, I had my 'that's sweet, but you're too young for me' speech all ready, but when he called I was so impressed!

In any case, it was a whirlwind courtship. Despite my best efforts, I was drawn to him. We saw each other every day. Since I was trying to "live right" and he was a minister (cha- ching – jackpot) we started off no kisses. We only hugged. He surprised me with an understanding, respectful spirit. We would sit out in the car for hours talking and holding hands. It got to the point that we hated leaving one another.

Late nights soon turned into days, weeks, months, etc. Then we were living together. That's when the trouble began...

I can't even remember what Conrad did to make me angry, but I do remember that I was on fire. I marched out of the bedroom and set an extra alarm clock on the dining room table in front of him. I remember saying something to the effect of him sleeping on the couch in the den. I expected that he would be upset and sleep out on the couch – all while calling me a five-letter explicative.

Sometime during the night I heard the bathroom light go on and him vomiting. I remember lying there thinking "Is this real?" I wondered if I should get up and go check on him. As I was about to go check on him, I thought that his ego might be bruised if I saw him at a moment like that. He, of course, did not feel that way. Instead, he felt that I had abandoned him in his time of need. This was the beginning of the end. Once he had determined that I could sleep without him and that I had left him "hanging" in the bathroom – his openness, trust, and belief were shattered.

Soon after, the rages began. Conrad would have fits of anger, tears, destruction, and suicide threats all during the wee hours of the morning. I have never been so frightened in all of my life. I would sometimes imagine that my body would be found bruised and battered. Perhaps I would be stabbed to death.

A rage was usually the result of a disagreement between the two of us. It would generally start off with Conrad feeling ignored. His feelings would be hurt and I would be tired and, therefore, evil and malicious. He would cry, and I would lie in the bed wishing that he would shut up and go to sleep. He would get up and go into the den, leave the apartment, come back, and then the rollercoaster ride to hell would begin around 2 or 3 a.m.

He would hit himself, put his head through walls, stab himself, grab me, curse me, etc. In the morning, I would be exhausted and unnerved by the previous night. Every time, I would question whether or not I was using common sense by continuing to be in this relationship. I thought to myself, "He's crazy." He put me in the mind of a wounded animal looking for love - jittery, panicky, and viciously trying to protect itself.

In those moments of fear and anxiety, I would beg God to take it all away. I would ask for forgiveness for making the wrong choices. I thought for sure that Conrad could not be from God – with his psychosis. Miraculously,

I would eventually have some peace even though the situation was miserable... I know that it's a sin that we live together, but I can help him.

THE DANGER OF DESIRE

In our drive to obtain our heart's desires, we often lose sight of God's desires for our lives. The Bible says that God foreknew us before the foundations of this world and predestined us for *his* purpose (Romans 8:29-30). God's plan for our life is perfect, "For I know the thoughts *and* plans that I have for you, says the Lord, thoughts *and* plans for welfare *and* peace and not of evil, to give you peace in your final outcome (Jeremiah 29:11 AMP)."

Kim allowed her desire for companionship to override the Holy Spirit. God will never require you to do something contrary to His Word in order to receive what he has for you. Being blessed will **never** involve you sinning. The Bible says:

> Let no one say when he is tempted, I am tempted by God; for God is incapable of being tempted by [what is] evil and He Himself tempts no one. But every person is tempted when he is drawn away and baited by his own evil desire (lust, passions) (James 1:13-14 AMP)."

The supreme tempter is the devil (Matthew 4:3, 1 Corinthians 7:5, 1 Thessalonians 3:5) who is able to play upon the weakness of corrupt human nature and lead people to destruction. The devil tempts, constantly, by using our desires against us. He tempts us by allowing our desires to appear to be just at our fingertips, but far enough away that it eludes our grasp. He seeks to make us resent the blessings that God has already given us as well as the blessings that he has in store for us, by focusing our attention on what we *don't* have.

God placed Adam in the Garden of Eden to work it and take care of it. God told Adam that he could eat from any tree in the garden, except the tree of the knowledge of good and evil (Genesis 2:15-16). When the serpent [the devil] approached Eve about the tree of the knowledge of good and evil, he tempted her with the desire to "be like God and know good and evil." In that moment, Eve did not focus on all the other trees that God had placed in the Garden of Eden for her and Adam, instead she focused on the one tree that God had forbidden them to eat from.

> "You will not surely die," the serpent said to the woman. "For God knows that when you eat of it your eyes will be opened, and you will be like God, knowing good and evil." When the woman saw that the

fruit of the tree was good for
food and pleasing to the eye,
and also desirable for gaining
wisdom, she took some and ate
it. She also gave some to her
husband, who was with her,
and he ate it (Genesis 3:4-6).

The Bible directs us to resist temptation, promising blessedness to those who do (James 1:12). It also directs us to pray for deliverance from exposure to temptation

---

The man that God sends
looking for you will not
require you to sin, by going
against God's Word, in order
to keep him.

---

and from surrender to it (Matthew 6:13, Luke 11:4). Remember that the Lord will not allow his children to encounter temptation beyond our Spirit-given ability to resist (1 Corinthians 10:13, 2 Peter 2:9). In essence, the man that God sends *looking for you* will not require you to sin, by going against God's Word, in order to keep him. For the Bible says, "He who *finds* a wife finds what is good and receives favor from the Lord (Proverbs 18:22, EMPHASIS ADDED)."

WHAT FRUIT?

The Bible says that you can tell a tree by the fruit that it bears, "...Do people pick grapes from thorn bushes, or figs from thistles? Likewise every good tree bears good fruit, but a bad tree bears bad fruit (Matthew 7:16-17)." Kim knew that her relationship with Conrad did not bear "good fruit."

Fornication, abuse, deceit, and manipulation are not of God. Many times we willingly allow someone to take advantage of us, or we justify remaining in a relationship that bears bad fruit so that we won't be lonely. Don't you know that you can be in a relationship and still be lonely? The only one who will never leave us nor forsake us, who can offer us comfort and supernatural peace is God. We will never be able to find in mortal men what God has offered us before our conception – unconditional love without compromise.

I was exhausted last night, I fell asleep around 4:15 a.m. I fell asleep on the floor next to the couch in the living room. Conrad awoke around 5:00 a.m., stepped over me and went to bed. At first, I was a little angry that he would just step over me and go get in the bed, but I was too tired to give it much thought.

Around 6:00 a.m. I got up and went to bed, too. Needless to say, this morning I was exhausted and did not go to work. Sooner or later something is going to have to give or I will lose my job. Things are still the same, if not worse. I have been praying to God during every incidence of Conrad's tears, convulsions, etc...to keep me.

I have asked God repeatedly to give me His heart for Conrad so that I can be compassionate and understanding. The problem is I don't know what's real and what's added drama. His sister, Michelle, who is a self-admitted drama queen, said she thought that he behaved the way that he did for attention. All I know is that I am so tired of everything. The good times are far and few between and the bad times are definitely bad!

I know that I can't continue much longer. It's like I'm in a bad dream – only I wake up and find myself right back in the same situation. I can't live the rest of my life this way. I called my maid of honor to tell her that the wedding was off if things don't get better.

I have to be honest; it's not all Conrad's fault. I just can't deal with the psychosis. Right at this very moment, Conrad is standing in front of the sliding glass doors that lead to the patio with no shirt on. Never mind the fact that it's about nineteen degrees outside and he just stepped out of the shower. He is purposely trying to make himself sick. I went back and forth with him about it, but ultimately decided that he's grown. If he wants to get sick so, be it. I refuse to let my positive attitude be stolen.

Frustrated that his attempt to hurt himself no longer elicits a response from me, Conrad retreated to the bedroom. After a while, he returned to say that he wanted to talk to me. As he talked, tears rolled down his face. He was crying. He told me that all he wanted to do was love me, but I keep rejecting him.

"My mother didn't want me and neither do you. You make me feel like I'm bothering you. You don't want me to touch you. You're beautiful. I can't help it. Every time I see you, I want to make love to you."

"It's not that I don't want to be with you. You know that I love you. I just don't want to continue living in sin. It's enough that we live together. I, at least, want to try to live right. Don't you feel guilty preaching about living right when you know that we don't?"

"There you go again. Using the Bible to try to hurt me. You're always throwing daggers at me!" Conrad said crying even harder.

"Conrad, I'm not throwing daggers at you. All I'm saying is I don't want to live like this anymore. I want to try to get back on track. You said that we would do that. You said that we would abstain from sex until we got married." Kim said pleading with him. The last thing that she wanted was to spark another rage in Conrad; he was so sensitive. Every time she opened up her mouth she felt like she was walking on eggshells.

"Just forget it." Conrad said as he walked away from her.

I did not realize how much I had hurt him, she wrote. I'm so insensitive that I originally thought that he was just too demanding; I thought that he over-dramatized everything. Lord, forgive me, I only think of myself. I can help him. Together, we can pray for deliverance to break the generational curses on his life. Kim and Conrad *were married six months later. They never received pre-marital counseling.*

SEEING RED

Many women feel the way that Kim did. "I can help him". In order to help someone, they must want to be helped. First, a person must recognize that they have a problem. Once they recognize that there's a problem they must have the desire to change and line up with the will of God. They must come to the point where they say to the Lord, "create in me a clean heart, O God, and renew a right, persevering, *and* steadfast spirit within me (Psalm 51:10 AMP). When we seek God with a sincere heart, he promises that we will find him (1 Chronicles 28:9).

Batterers come from all walks of life, but the general characteristics of a batterer include the following: A batterer objectifies women. He does not see women as people. He does not respect women as a group. Overall, women are viewed as property or sexual objects. In general, batterers have low-self esteem. He often feels powerless and ineffective in the world. He may appear confident and successful, but inside he feels inadequate. A Batterer doesn't take responsibility for his actions.

God does not intend for his daughters to be in abusive relationships with men who are unable to cover and/or love their wives in the manner in which he has called them.

Instead, he makes excuses and externalizes his behavior. He blames his violence on stress, his partner's behavior, or other factors. In most cases, a batterer is pleasant and charming between periods of violence. Therefore, he is often seen as a "nice guy" to outsiders.

God does not intend for his daughters to be in abusive relationships with men who are unable to cover and/or love their wives in the manner in which he has called them. In fact, God despises the mistreatment of wives by their husbands (Colossians 3:19, 1 Peter 3:7, Ephesians 5:25-33).

The best way to prevent ending up feeling trapped in an abusive marriage is to get to know a person before making the commitment to marry. Abusive characteristics are manifested in one's personality. These "red flags" are always there, but are often overlooked or even ignored when attraction and infatuation take over. These signs can include irrational jealousy, the need to be in control, a quick temper, attempts to isolate the other person from his or her friends and family, drug or alcohol abuse, and disrespect for their partner's boundaries, privacy, personal space, or moral values.

REFLECTION QUESTIONS

1. Which desires have caused you to lose sight of God's intentions for your life?

2. How has the devil tempted you with these desires?

3. What steps have you taken to resist these temptations?

4. What are you looking for in man that you can only find in God?

5. What "red flags" have you been able to identify?

CHAPTER TWO

RESCUE 911

Gloria is saved, sanctified, and on fire for the Lord. She is the Youth Leader at her church and regularly participates with the mission ministry by going out and evangelizing in the inner city neighborhoods. Gloria is a virtuous woman of God.

Most of Gloria's friends are saved, but aren't necessarily living for God. Gloria doesn't judge them, because the Bible says that, "There is only one Lawgiver and Judge, the one who is able to save and destroy. But you – who are you to judge your neighbor (James 4:12)?" Instead, she tries to be a godly example and minister to them as the Lord leads.

One night, she was visiting with one of her married girlfriends, Stephanie, and that's when she met David.

David works with Stephanie's husband Keith. The guys had come home after playing a couple of games of basketball. Stephanie made dinner for the hungry twosome and Gloria and David hit it right off.

There were so many redeeming qualities about David. He was laid-back, well educated, hard working, and established. He had never been married and had no kids! He was moderately attractive and appeared to have his "stuff" together. There was one problem, he didn't know Jesus.

Gloria surmised that although this could be catastrophic, it could also be her opportunity to witness to the man that she could one day marry. After all, she thought, God has used me to bring several people to him – to accept Jesus as their Lord and Savior. I will pray that through my witness, David will be saved, also.

UNEQUALLY YOKED & VULNERABLE

Women, the first mistake that we make is to entertain a relationship with a man who is not saved. The first prerequisite that we have as women of virtue is to save ourselves for a godly man. When we enter into relationship with someone who does not share our beliefs regarding God, we place ourselves in a vulnerable position and leave room for the devil to come in and tempt us away from God.

In the Old Testament, when God entered into a covenant with Moses and the children of Israel, He warned Moses not to enter into agreement with the Amorites, Canaanites, Hittites, Perizzites, Hivites and

Jebusites, "Be careful not to make treaty with those who live in the land; for when they prostitute themselves to their gods and sacrifice to them, they will invite you and you will eat their sacrifices. And when you choose some of their daughters as wives for your sons and those daughters prostitute themselves to their gods, they will lead your sons to do the same (Exodus 34:12, 15-16)."

God reiterated this command, again, in Deuteronomy 7: 3-4, "Do not intermarry with them. Do not give your daughters to their sons or take their daughters for your sons, for they will turn your sons away from following me to serve other gods, and the Lord's anger will burn against you and will quickly destroy you." Intermarriage with the Canaanite people would have tempted the Israelites to adopt Canaanite culture and customs. Thus, they were commanded not to blend in, but to be set apart as God's chosen people.

Solomon is an example of a man whose heart was turned away from God when he intermarried. Solomon was the son of David and succeeded his father as king of Israel. God appeared to Solomon in a dream and told him that whatever he asked for, God would give it to him. Instead of asking for riches and honor, Solomon asked for a discerning heart and wisdom in order to judge the people of Israel. God was pleased with Solomon's request and promised to give him a wise and discerning heart, "Moreover, I will give you what you have not asked for – both riches and honor- so that in your lifetime you will have no equal among kings. And if you walk in my ways and obey my statues as David your father did, I will give you a long life (I Kings 3:10-1)."

---

*W*e are called to minister to individuals who don't know Christ, not to marry them.

Sadly, toward the end of his lfe, Solomon became restless and ungratified. His greatest sin was losing devotion to God. In this, he fell victim to his own trade agreements. By custom, beautiful women were given to the most powerful member of a treaty to seal the covenant. As a result, Solomon had a constant influx of wives and concubines. He allowed his concubines and wives to practice their pagan religions and this eventually led to his downfall. Solomon's own faith was weakened and he ultimately approved of and participated in idolatrous acts (I Kings 11:1-13).

This is why it is crucial that we not put ourselves in a position where our hearts can be turned away from God. We are called to minister to individuals who don't know Christ, not to marry them. When in doubt, consult the Bible for guidance. The devil studies us and knows what we desire. The Bible says that the devil roams the earth like a lion seeking whom he can devour (1 Peter 5:8). Don't make yourself an easy target by disobeying God in this matter. This topic is even re-visited in the

New Testament when Paul warned the Corinthians not to be unequally yoked together with an unbeliever:

> Do not be unequally yoked with unbelievers [do not make mismated alliances with them or come under a different yoke with them, inconsistent with your faith]. For what partnership have right living *and* right standing with God and iniquity *and* lawlessness? Or how can light have fellowship with darkness?...Or what has a believer in common with an unbeliever?...So, come out from among [unbelievers], and separate (sever) yourselves from them, says the Lord...(2 Corinthians 6:14-17 AMP).

Yoked comes from the Greek word heterozugeo (het-er-od-zoog-eh´-o) which means to associate discordantly (conflicting, clashing, contrary). Many of us would not be in the relationships that we are in today had we just obeyed the Word of God.

Gloria was on cloud nine. Things were, for all intents and purposes, going well with her and David. Their relationship was progressing and she had hoped that she would be receiving a marriage proposal soon.

Over the past year, the two had vacationed together and spent almost every free moment that they had together. Gloria was pleased to finally be in a committed relationship. She often grilled her married girls to get "helpful tid-bits" to prepare her for married life.

"Marriage isn't easy." Stephanie told her sternly. "Keith and I work very hard at making our marriage work. Marriage is truly a ministry. As a wife, you have to learn to submit to your husband and respect him no matter how you may disagree with the decisions that he may sometimes make. Single women are running, jumping, and plain overanxious about getting married. Wait on God! He will prepare you for the Man of God that He has for you", she said as she turned to place her hand on Gloria's arm as if to physically restrain her.

"I'm ready." Gloria responded confidently. "I believe that God has sent David to me. Waiting is easy for you to say because you have a husband and children. You have a family. You have someone to share your dreams and aspirations with. You have someone to put their arms around you and tell you things will be all right when you wake up, startled, in the middle of the night. I want that, too. I want someone to spend the rest of my life with." Gloria said longingly.

Gloria knew that Stephanie was just trying to look - out for her best interest, but she had alreudy prayed about her situation. Well, maybe not prayed, but she had at least made her desires known to God. She wanted to be a wife and a mother. Doesn't every little girl dream about her wedding, husband, and children? Gloria wanted it all - two kids, white picket fence, and a dog!

While she and David had been getting along okay, there was still a slight glitch. Yes, glitch was a nice way to put it, because it could be rectified...

David was still not saved. She had asked, even begged him to go to church with her. He had gone a few times early in their relationship, but he showed no true interest in being in church nor a desire to come to know Christ. Gloria continued to pray for God to prick David, but David didn't budge.

Gloria noticed that talking about church and God made David uncomfortable.

"I would never have gone out with you if I knew that you were a 'Church Fanatic'", David said. "Get off my back about it. I don't like your church and I don't want to go. I'm going to watch the game over my dude's house. Call me when you get home. Oh, and I'm not interested in hearing the service so you can bypass the tape ministry this Sunday and every Sunday!" He said as he kissed her on the cheek and walked out the door.

However, Gloria kept telling herself that things would change.

"Eventually he will come around. I'll just keep on praying. After all, the Bible says that the 'Prayers of a righteous man availeth much'", she thought.

Three months later David proposed to Gloria and

she said, yes.

　　　David was still not saved.

ENABLING OR SAVING?

The second mistake that we make is believing that we can "save him." It is very important that, as women, we come to the understanding, once and for all, that the only Savior is Jesus Christ. Only the blood of the lamb offers salvation. More often than not, we compromise our own walk and get in the Lord's way. Instead of ministering, we enable individuals – friends, family members, our spouse, and/or our children - to stay in the valley. The American Heritage Dictionary defines enable (v) as:

1. **a.** To supply with the means, knowledge, or opportunity to be or do something.
   b. To make feasible or possible. **2.** To give legal power, capacity, or sanction to.

Stop sacrificing your walk, your relationship with God, and your testimony in efforts to try to "save" a man. God is God all by Himself and He doesn't require our help. Instead, He only requires our obedience, "... Does the Lord delight in burnt offerings and sacrifices as much as in obeying the voice of the Lord? To obey is better than sacrifice, and to heed is better than the fat of rams. For rebellion is like the sin of divination, and arrogance like the evil of idolatry...(1 Samuel 15:22-

23)."

REFLECTION QUESTIONS

1. What dangers are associated with being unequally yoked?

2. How have you allowed your heart to be turned away from God?

3. What behaviors have you been enabling your partner to continue? In what way(s)?

4. How has your walk with God been affected by your relationship?

CHAPTER THREE

AGAPE LOVE?

Veronica and Mike have been together since the ninth grade. She was a cheerleader and he was on the football team. They had dreamed of attending college together, but that was before the birth of Little Mike during their senior year of high school. Both of them grew up without having a relationship with their father and consequently were determined not to let the same thing happen to their own son.

Immediately following high school graduation, while their friends were planning family vacations and college shopping sprees, Veronica and Mike were planning to move in to a two-bedroom apartment together with their infant son. Thankfully, Veronica's mother had been able to get her a job at the bank where she worked as a full-time customer service representative. Mike, on the other hand, wanted to make "fast" money. He was interested in providing for his family, as well as, keeping up with the "boys."...

The last four years have been extremely difficult for Veronica. The loss of her mother in a fatal car crash last year and the stress of having three children at the age of twenty-four have greatly taken a toll on her. However, money is no object these days as Mike's "hustle" is at its peak. Both of them drive luxury cars and wear designer clothing. Materially, they want for nothing. Of course, with money comes power and Mike has no problem exerting his power over his young wife.

===================

Once again, a simple disagreement had sent Mike into a rage. Veronica was concerned about the little old lady who lived in the apartment directly under theirs. She had called the police on Veronica and Mike in the past. Veronica thought that after tonight they would either be evicted or Mike would be in jail. "What excuse will I give the police now?" She thought. Veronica, tired of arguing and sensing trouble, had gone into the bedroom to get ready for bed. She was relieved that he didn't follow her in there as he normally did.

Later, in the night, smelling of alcohol and weed, Mike awakened her with a gun to her head. In the past, he has slapped her around, pushed her or called her a fat whore or bitch, but this night, he held the gun to her *head and threatened to kill her for not listening to him.*

"You're just like my mother", he cried. "She would always push me to these limits and then when I went off she would want to listen to me, suddenly, understanding where I was coming from."

Throughout the night Veronica would plead and cry for her life – for his life, too.

Mike eventually calmed down, apologized, and professed his love for her. After making love to Veronica and before passing out he muttered, "Girl, you know I love you. You just make me crazy sometimes. You know I can't live without you...I'd kill you if you ever tried to leave me."

Sometimes, when she had a moment of peace, she couldn't help but think, "What have I gotten myself into?" She loved him and, despite the abuse, she knew that he truly loved her. Mike just had a rough upbringing. His drug-addicted mother had physically and verbally abused him as a child. He claimed that she would often leave her young children to fend for and raise themselves while she fed her drug addiction. He didn't know how to love. He told Veronica that he had never been loved the way that she loved him.

If we were honest, we would all say that at some point or another we have asked ourselves the question, "How did I get here?" We fervently search our minds and retrace our steps in our effort to remember every detail of the decision making process that landed us in our current situation.

Some of us blame our situations on "love". We would say that we were so in love that we could not see what was right in front of us. I submit that, rather, we refused to see or adhere to the warning signals because we were in love with the idea of what the world views as "love".

"Love" what exactly does it mean? When you say that you "love" someone or something, what are you really saying? Love is perhaps the most misused word in the English language. We use it to describe our feelings about food, material possessions, shoes and clothing, etc. The word "love" has been thrown around so much that it's lost its true meaning.

The American Heritage Dictionary defines love as:

> *n.* **1.a.** An intense affection for another person based on familial or personal ties. **b.** A strong affection for or attachment to another person based on regard or shared experiences or interests. **2.** An expression of one's affection: send him my love. **3. a.** An intense attraction to another person based largely on sexual desire. **b.** The deep affection, tenderness, and concern felt for a person with whom one has or

wishes to have a relationship based on sexual attraction. **c.** The person who is the object of such an attraction; beloved.

Regardless of economics, race or status, people value love. Ultimately, we believe that love will shape what is good and true. In our society, love permeates and lies at the heart of everything. Since our English word love is used so broadly, we need to distinguish between the different types of love in order to gain a more precise understanding of the Bible's command to love.

EROS

Eros is probably what most people mean when they announce with a smile, "I'm in love." This type of love covers everything from queasy stomachs and warm fuzzy feelings to strong sensual passion.

*A*lthough eros at times might make us feel like we are on cloud nine, it can not provide a reliable basis for building a deep and meaningful relationship.

There are a couple of very interesting characteristics about eros. First, in order to exist, eros *is dependent upon* the situation and circumstances. As long as a couple is enjoying a romantic situation, eros can thrive. But, as soon as hurtful words or actions appear, eros simply evaporates.

Second, eros is defined by each person's perception. For example, if someone perceives a particular quiet evening dinner with candles to be romantic, eros will thrive. However, passion becomes squashed for someone whenever he or she interprets the current situation to be undesirable. Eros will either survive and grow stronger, or die and fade away based upon our perceptions.

Although eros at times might make us feel like we are on cloud nine, *it can not provide a reliable basis for building a deep and meaningful relationship* since it is so fickle and dependent upon perception and circumstances. Because of such things as accidents, diseases, and life's circumstances overall, it is clear that we can not determine how others will perceive us nor are we masters of our own circumstances. Although eros is exhilarating, this is not the Biblical word used for love.

GOD'S LOVE

Love is the high esteem which God has for His children and the high regard which they, in turn, should have for Him and other people. Because of the hundreds of references to love in the Bible, it is certainly the most remarkable book of love in the world. It records the greatest love story ever written – God's unconditional love for us that sent His son to die on the cross (John 3:16, 1 John 4:10).

> For God so greatly loved *and* dearly prized the world that He [even] gave up His only begotten (*b*unique) Son, so that whoever believes in (trusts in, clings to, relies on) Him shall not perish (come to destruction, be lost), but have eternal (everlasting) life. For God did not send the Son into the world in order to judge (to reject, to condemn, to pass sentence on) the world, but that the world might find salvation *and* be made safe *and* sound through Him (1 John 3:16-17 AMP).

Two Greek words for love appear in the Bible. Depending on the context, they may express distinct meanings. *Phileo* can mean "to have ardent affection and feeling", while *agapao* can denote "to have esteem" or "high regard."

PHILIA

We recognize philia from the name Philadelphia, that is, the city of brotherly love. This is the love of friendship, best friends, and the fellowship of being with those people you enjoy.

Although philia is wonderful, it is not reliable since it is also dependent on circumstances and, can be manipulated by our and other's perceptions and expectations.

Unfortunately, we probably all know of a friendship which waned or was severed because of time, distance, harsh words, misinterpretation of one's actions/motives, etc.

When the New Testament commands love, philia is the not the word which is used.

Agape

Unlike the previous two types of love, agape is not limited to expectations and/or perception. Agape is based upon the commitment to proactively seek someone else's well being.

Agape love conveys God's will to His children about their attitude toward one another. Love for one another is proof to the world of true discipleship (John 13:34-35). Agape love expresses the essential nature of God (1 John 4:9-10) because love finds its perfect expression in the Lord Jesus. Christian love is the fruit of the Spirit of Jesus in the believer (Galatians 5:22).

> Love [agape] is patient and
> kind. Love is not jealous or
> boastful or proud or rude. Love
> does not demand its own way.

> Love is not irritable, and keeps
> no record of when it has been
> wronged. It is never glad about
> injustice but rejoices whenever
> the truth wins out. Love never
> gives up, never loses faith, is
> always hopeful, and endures
> through every circumstance (1
> Corinthians 13:4-7).

Since it is neither a knee jerk reaction nor just a responsive feeling to how we've been treated, agape is capable of existing despite dire and hostile circumstances. Agape love can even survive in an environment where there are no warm fuzzy feelings. For example, Jesus' teaching that we should agape our enemies is intended to show the boundless nature of the Christian commitment toward seeking another's well-being (Luke 6:35).

The New Testament is full of examples and teachings illustrating the nature of agape as well as training the disciple's heart to be shaped by agape. A few of these teachings which underline the active nature of agape include...

> Knowing that sinful man would kill His Son, but also knowing that without Jesus we were doomed, God loved us by sending his Son (John 3:16).

❧ Those who love Jesus will do what Jesus taught (John 14:15, 23).

❧ If a person has material resources and the love of God within him, his heart will take care of his brother who is in need (1 John 3:17).

❧ Just as Christ through love acted on behalf of the church, so too the Christian husband is to be motivated by love to act on behalf of his wife. Ephesians 5:25-29

Not only can the proactive power and nature of agape rise above its environment, but it can also empower passion and friendship. For example, when a spouse chooses to speak and act toward their mate with agape, this creates the loving environment in which eros and philia can thrive.

---

*W*hen we define love, it
is absolutely crucial that we
use God's definition and not
the world's.

Although this spouse might even perceive the other spouse as being unkind or rude, responding out of agape nurtures the growth of the other forms of love. This can prevent additional problems.

When God commanded us to agape love one another, it was not His intention that we allow ourselves to be mistreated and abused in the process. Yes, as Christians, we understand that we need to forgive and turn the other cheek (Matthew 5:39, Luke 6:29) and to continue to love despite the offense because the Bible says that love covers a multitude of sins (1 Peter 4:8).

However, God did not intend for our relationships to be abusive. Love does not allow for jealousy, envy, pride, a haughty spirit, selfishness, rudeness, a demand for one's own way, irritability, nor grudges. The Bible says that, "Love must be sincere. Hate what is evil; cling to what is good. Be devoted to one another in brotherly love. Honor one another above yourselves (Romans 12:9,10)." When we define love, it is absolutely crucial that we use God's definition and not the world's.

REFLECTION QUESTIONS

1. What does the word "love" mean to you? How do you define it?

2. What type of "love" does your relationship exhibit?

3. How does agape love differ from that love?

4. How did Christ exemplify agape love?

5. As a body of believers, how can we better show agape love to each other and the world?

PART II

STANDING ON GOD'S WORD

My sheep listen to my voice; I know
them, and they follow me
John 10:27

CHAPTER FOUR

<u>What Does the Bible Say?</u>

Gloria and David were married for almost three years and things were getting worse instead of better. David's true colors began to emerge about six months after the marriage...

─────────────

David, a banker by trade, had faced some challenges with regard to being able to maintain employment. Three months after they were married, David was fired from his job for tardiness and excessive absences. Gloria was shocked because he left the house for work at the same time every morning. She couldn't understand how he could have been late much less miss work all together.

"What do you mean they fired you because you

were late?" Gloria asked. None of this was making any sense to her.

"Babe, just let it go. They fired me. End of story!" David shot back.

"You leave the house every morning at the same time that I do. Explain to me how you were late, much less absent."

"Listen, there were a couple of times that I didn't make it in to the office because I had some business to take care of. Don't worry about it. I'll get anther job, damn."

Gloria knew that she wasn't going to get anywhere with this conversation. She wasn't stupid. David wasn't telling her the truth, but she also knew that when he got all defensive that things could escalate quickly, and she didn't want to go there today.

That wouldn't be the last time David would lie to Gloria. As it turned out, David wasn't very responsible. While they were dating, it appeared that he had it all together (although, there were some 'red flags'). For starters, David ran through money like water. If he had any money when he left the house in the morning, you could bet that it would be gone by the time he came back to the house that night.

Things got so bad that Gloria had to take the ATM card from him so that she could keep money in their joint checking account. Secondly, the boy was a dreamer. The only thing that he was interested in was becoming a multi-millionaire. The problem, he didn't have a strategy as to how to become a millionaire. What Gloria soon learned was that David was a good talker, but follow-through was something that he knew nothing about.

Gloria tried to be supportive of David. They spent several thousand dollars on his music career. David wanted to produce hip-hop. Certainly, he had a love for music, but Gloria wasn't sure that he had what it took to set himself apart as a producer. In fact, she discovered that spending excessive amounts of time at the studio is what got him fired from his job at the bank. Every time his artist called (a.k.a. his boy "Killa"), David hopped up to run to the studio.

"David, Killa doesn't have a job, you just can't go running to the studio every time he calls."

"You knew that I had dreams and aspirations when you met me. Once we get Killa signed everything will be o.k. Go fix yourself a sandwich or something. I don't have time to try to explain this to your fat ass. Eating is the only thing you seem to understand anyway."

"You don't have to insult me; I was only trying to look out for you!" Gloria was used to the jabs at her weight. She had gained about thirty pounds since they had gotten married and David was very vocal about his dissatisfaction with her weight gain.

"All I'm saying is, if you can't support me, then I can find someone who will. Women throw themselves at me all the time, baby. You just don't understand. Other women think that you have it made. Why do you always have to find something to complain about?"

In truth, Gloria was afraid of losing David. All in all, they lived a comfortable life. David was able to hustle *up enough jobs as a producer to keep their bills paid and some money in the bank. They had just bought a new home and had been discussing starting a family. Perhaps she was complaining too much. After all the Bible says that it's "Better to live in a desert than with a quarrelsome and ill-tempered wife (Proverbs 21:19)."*

They had a decent relationship, but Gloria felt like they were growing apart instead of together. David spent the majority of his time at work, and whatever free time he had, with artists in the studio. Gloria craved attention from her husband. She constantly asked him when they were going to be able to spend time together.

"Gloria, I have to keep working in order to keep the bills paid and food on the table."

"I know, but when are you going to make time for us? What about starting a family? You said that you were ready to have a baby."

"I do want to start working on having a family, but you have got to lose some weight first. I'm finding it difficult to even be attracted to you right now."

"If you weren't spending all your time in the studio with all those underage, half-dressed, fast-tail girls maybe you might be able to spend some quality time with your wife."

"Either you're going to lose some weight, or we won't be having no babies because you won't be having me!"

Gloria ran into her bedroom and slammed the door behind her. She couldn't believe that David had said that he wasn't attracted to her anymore. Hot tears rolled down her face. What happened to "in good times and bad, until death do us part?" As she thought about her dream of becoming a mother, she cried even harder.

WHAT IS MARRIAGE?

Marriage is the union of a man and a woman as husband and wife. Marriage was instituted by God when he declared, " It is not good that man should be alone; I will make him a helper comparable to him" (Gen. 2:18). So God fashioned woman and brought her to man. When Adam saw Eve he said, "This is now bone of my bone and flesh of my flesh and she shall be called Woman, because she was taken out of Man (Gen. 2:23)." This passage also emphasizes the truth that "a man shall leave his father and mother and be joined to his wife, and they shall become one flesh (Gen. 2:24)." This confirms the idea that God created a man to be the husband of one wife and for the marriage to be life long.

Marriage should not be entered into lightly, but rather through prayer and seeking God's will for your life.

Marriage is a covenant between you, your spouse, and God. The marriage covenant is formal, public, legal, and sacred – a binding contract. You have committed, before God, to *agape* love your spouse. Therefore, marriage should not be entered into lightly, but rather through prayer and seeking God's will for your life. Certainly, marriage requires dying to self, daily, so that our love will be self-less as Jesus' love for us was when he died on the cross for our sins.

Marriage is the outward manifestation of how Christ loved the church. Christ loved the church so much that he gave up his desires, his dreams of a natural life, his opinions, his thoughts, and his life for us so that whoever believes in him will not perish, but have eternal life (John 3:16). Consequently, the devil will always seek to destroy the institution of marriage because of what it represents to the world.

INSTRUCTIONS FOR HUSBANDS AND WIVES

God calls husbands and wives to subject themselves to one another out of esteem for God (Ephesians 5:21). Wives are commanded to honor their husbands, "Wives, be subject (be submissive and adapt yourselves) to your own husbands as [a service] to the Lord (Ephesians 5:22 AMP).

Submission

The Greek word for submission is **hupŏtassō** (hoop-ot-aś-so) which means to put under, subdue unto, (be, make), put into subjection (to, under), submit self unto. It does not refer to being under the absolute control of another, but rather to voluntarily place oneself under the authority of another. Just as Christ is not inferior to the Father, but is the second Person in the Trinity, so wives are equal to their own husbands. Husbands and wives have different roles in the marriage. God has ordained the wife's role to be one of voluntary submission to her husband that is born out of her submission to Christ.

And husbands are instructed to love their wives as Christ loved the church:

> For the husband is the head of the wife as Christ is the Head of the church, Himself the Savior of [His] body. As the church is subject to Christ, so let wives be subject in everything to their husbands. Husbands, love your wives, as Christ loved the church and gave himself up for her, So that he might sanctify her, having cleansed her by the washing of water with the Word, That He might present the church to Himself in glorious splendor, without spot or wrinkle or any such things [that she might be holy and faultless]. Even so husbands should love their wives as [being in a sense] their

own bodies. He who loves his own wife loves himself. For no man ever hated his own flesh, but nourishes and carefully protects and cherishes it, as Christ does the church (Ephesians 5:23-29 AMP).

The man is the head of the wife, Christ is the head of the man, and God is the head of Jesus (1 Corinthians 11:3). As the head of the family, husbands are expected to assume spiritual, social, and economical responsibility for their family. The husband, as the head, is responsible for the spiritual well-being of his family. The husband is supposed to wash his wife with the word so that she will be holy and faultless just as Jesus' crucifixion on the cross sanctified the church.

In the Old Testament, husbands functioned as the priest of their family by sacrificing on their family's behalf (Genesis 12:8, Job 1:5). Later, when priesthood was established in Israel, the husband's role was redefined as the spiritual leader in the home. As such, he was responsible for rearing his children in godliness (Exodus 12:3, 26-27, Proverbs 22:6, Ephesians 6:4).

Socially, a husband is responsible for making sure that no one takes advantage of his family. And economically, he is also responsible for providing for the financial needs of his family as well. The Bible says that "If anyone does not provide for his relatives, and especially for his immediate family, he has denied the faith and is worse than an unbeliever (1 Timothy 5:8)." A believer is to provide for his near relatives and his immediate family. If a Christian cannot even care for his own family, how can that person love and care for others as God has called us to do?

CONTEMPTIBLE TREATMENT

While the Bible does not reference domestic violence, specifically, it does speak to God's disdain for a husband who mistreats his wife. For example, a husband who does not treat his wife with respect is in jeopardy of not having his prayers answered. "In the same way you married men should live considerately with [your wives], with intelligent recognition [of the marriage relation], honoring the woman as [physically] the weaker, but [realizing that you] are joint heirs of the grace (God's unmerited favor) of life, in order that your prayers may not be hindered *and* cut off. [Otherwise you cannot pray effectively.] (1 Peter 3:7 AMP).

Furthermore, God speaks of His displeasure with men who treat their wives treacherously in the second chapter of the Book of Malachi. When the subject of divorce is mentioned, the most popular verse quoted by Christians is Malachi 3:16, God hates divorce. However, in an effort to understand that verse better, let's take a look at the verses that proceed verse sixteen:

> 13 And this you do with double guilt; you cover the alter of the Lord with tears [shed by

your offending wives, divorced by you that you might take heathen wives[, and with [your own] weeping and crying out because the Lord does not regard your offering any more or accept it with favor at your hand.

[14] Yet you ask, Why does he reject it? Because the Lord was witness [to the covenant made at your marriage] between you and the wife of your youth, against whom you have dealt treacherously and to who you were faithless. Yet she is your companion and the wife of your covenant [made by your marriage vows].

[15] And did not God make [you and your wife] one [flesh]? Did not One make you and preserve your spirit alive? and why [did God make you two] one? Because He sought a godly offspring [from your union]. Therefore take heed to yourselves, and let no one deal treacherously and be faithless to the wife of his youth (Malachi

3:13-15).

The Book of Malachi is a short prophetic book of the Old Testament written to rebuke the people of Israel for their shallow worship practices. The people had become apathetic towards God and this was reflected in their offerings to God as well as their relations with their spouses. It had become common at this time for men to divorce their wives. They ignored the fact that the Lord had witnessed their marriages. In turn, God ignored their sacrifices.

---

*G*od not only hates divorce, but he also hates a man who covers his wife with violence.

Verses thirteen through sixteen speak to the husband's consequences for mistreating their wives. The men were upset because God was ignoring their sacrifices. The Bible tells us that when the right things are done for the wrong reasons or with the wrong attitudes, God does not accept them (Psalm 40:6-8).

These men not only remarried pagan wives, but they divorced their first wives in order to make room for and marry their new wives. To the Lord, attitudes of indifference (apathy, unimportance, inferiority) to marriage vows and duties are the actions of a traitor (two-timer, betrayer, defector).

> [16] For the Lord , the God of Israel, says: I hate divorce and marital separation *and him who covers his garment [his wife] with violence*. Therefore keep a watch upon your spirit [that it may be controlled by My Spirit], that you deal not treacherously and faithlessly [with your marriage mate] (Malachi 3:16, AMP, EMPHASIS ADDED).

God not only hates divorce, but he also hates a man who covers his wife with violence. The Hebrew word for violence, in this verse, is **châmâç** (khaw-mawce´) which means to wrong; unjust gain – cruel (ty), damage, false, injustice, oppressor, unrighteous, violence (against, done), violent (dealing), wrong. The root word of **châmâç** (khaw-mas´) means to be violent; to maltreat – make bare, shake off violate, do violence, take away violently, wrong, imagine wrongfully. So if God hates for a man to treat his wife *violently*, then, clearly, God despises domestic violence.

God does hate divorce. God intends for marriage to be a lifelong bond that unites husband and wife in a "one flesh" relationship (Matthew 19:6). This is why God warns us not to be unequally yoked with unbelievers.

To the rest I say this (I, not the Lord); If any brother has a wife who is not a believer and she is willing to live with him, he must not divorce her. And if a woman has a husband who is not a believer and he is willing to live with her, she must not divorce him. For the unbelieving husband has been sanctified through his wife, and the unbelieving wife has been sanctified through her believing husband...***But if the unbeliever leaves, let him do so. A believing man or woman is not bound in such circumstances; God has called us to live in peace*** (1 Corinthians 7:12-15, EMPHASIS ADDED).

Ultimately God loves us and desires for us to live in peace, "...Everyone who loves has been born of God and knows God. Whoever does not love does not know God, because God is love...No one has ever seen God; but if we love one another, God lives in us and his love is made complete in us (1 John 4:7-12). When husbands don't love their wives like Christ loves the church, then the marriage is doomed to fail, "Under three things the earth trembles, under four it cannot bear up: ... an unloved woman who is married... (Proverbs 30:21-23)."

REFLECTION QUESTIONS

1. Why is it important to seek God through prayer before getting married?

2. Why does the devil seek to destroy the institution of marriage

3. Define submission as it relates to God's instructions to wives.

4. What does it mean for a man to love his wife as Christ loved the church? List five (5) examples.

5. What consequences exist for a man who mistreats his wife?

CHAPTER FIVE

<u>Hearing From God for Myself</u>

Things had gotten really tight since they had Jordan. Kim's job was so stressful that she quit it during her eighth month and decided to stay home and take care of the baby. Things between her and Conrad were as strained as ever. He was never at home and Kim felt like she was going through her pregnancy and their marriage by herself. She had never been so lonely in her life.

This was supposed to be a happy time in her life, wasn't it? She and Conrad had just moved into their very first home and now they were expecting their first child. The only problem, Conrad was MIA (missing in action).

He didn't seem to take an interest in Kim nor his unborn child. The violent episodes continued. Conrad even attacked Kim when she was six weeks pregnant...

═══════════════

Kim and Conrad had issues with the closing of their new home. Consequently they had to move out of their apartment and into their new home in haste to avoid having to pay another month's rent.

They had also just learned that Kim was expecting. Unfortunately, Kim had miscarried in the past. So when she began cramping while packing up the apartment she became worried. Kim rushed to the emergency room. Thankfully, she found out that everything was okay and her pregnancy was progressing normally. Their apartment, however, was in total chaos. So Kim decided to go there after she left the hospital to finish packing up. Kim's mother, Jean, met her at the apartment to help her finish packing.

"You know that you shouldn't be here packing. You're pregnant."

"I know, mom, but it has to get done."

"Why can't Conrad do it?" Jean did not like the way Conrad treated Kim. She didn't trust him and she felt like Kim had made a grave mistake by marrying him. He was never at home and Kim could never depend on him.

"Mom, let's not get into it. He said he would do it, but you know that I can't depend on him."

No sooner than Kim got the words out of her mouth,

the key turned in the lock of the apartment door. Conrad stormed into the apartment demanding that Kim go home.

"What are you doing here? Didn't I tell you that I was going to take care of this?" Conrad said, as he stood directly in front of Kim's face.

"I know what you said, but I wanted to make sure that it got done." Kim stated matter-of-factly.

"You enjoy making me look like a fool in front of your mother, don't you? Get your stuff and go home now!"

Kim silently prayed that Jean would not interject. She could tell from the look on Conrad's face that he was in the midst of a temper tantrum. Jean was not a woman to hold her tongue and she didn't have a problem getting down and dirty. Thankfully, Jean kept right on packing as if they weren't there.

"I'll leave when I get done." Kim did her best to remain calm and keep her voice even.

In an instant, Conrad had grabbed her arms and had her pinned up against the wall.

"No, You're going home now!"

"Get your hands off my daughter!" Jean had run to lodge herself in between Kim and Conrad. She was trying to use her weight to push Conrad off of Kim.

"Mom, step back and stay out of this. Conrad take your hands off of my mother." It took everything in Kim to give the appearance that she was calm when inside she was freaking out because things had escalated in front of and involving her mother!

"Fine. Do what you want." Conrad released her and stormed out of the apartment slamming the door behind him.

That night when Kim returned to their new home, Conrad was there waiting. Kim was on the phone with Jean, ignoring Conrad. Enraged, Conrad slapped her so hard that the phone went flying across the room. As she scrambled to her feet, there he was trying to calm her down.

"Shut up, the neighbors will hear you. You're going to get me in trouble!" Conrad screamed hysterically as his grip tightened around her throat.

Kim's arms went flailing in the air and her fist caught Conrad across his jaw. Suddenly his grip loosened and he began apologizing.

"I'm sorry. I'm sorry."

"Get out!" Kim was hysterical. The only thing that she could think about was her unborn child.

Jean had been on the phone the entire time. When she heard all of the commotion she and Jackson, Kim's father, rushed over to Kim's house. Jean knew that Conrad had a terrible temper, but she had no idea that things had become physical. Jackson made Conrad leave. Conrad stayed away for two weeks and then he and Kim reconciled...

═══════════════════

It was a week before Christmas and Jordan was eight weeks old. Conrad had asked Kim what she wanted for Christmas and since money was almost non-existent she said nothing. Earlier in the month they had fallen out, and he had taken some money out of their checking account and left for a week. Thus a couple of the checks that Kim had written for bills had bounced and caused their bills to fall behind.

They were in bad shape financially and otherwise. Their car payment was behind and Kim planned on asking her parents to help out, again, and loan them the money to pay their bills. The relationship between Kim and Conrad was in as bad a repair as their finances. Kim and Conrad had not been intimate for approximately seven months., Conrad had not had an interest in her, sexually, since she became pregnant with Jordan.

"I have decided that for Christmas I want to spend a romantic weekend with my husband." Kim smiled suggestively.

"I'm really not on sex anymore. I haven't had any in so long that it doesn't even matter to me. Besides, I have a lot on my mind, right now. Sex just ain't important."

Kim could not believe what she was hearing. Conrad was twenty-seven years old. Not interested in sex? Yeah, right! This is the same man who used to go into a rage when I said that I didn't want to make love until we got married. This is also the same man who came home with a condom in his pocket last week!

Kim's was furious! Not only did she feel ignored, but now unwanted. I'll be damned if I'm going to be married and be lonely – continuing to be horny for no other reason than he "isn't on that" right now. Bull shit! She thought.

Kim started cleaning the house. Whenever she got angry she began to clean. Cleaning gave her something to do with all of her negative energy. It helped her to clam down. As she cleaned the kitchen she angrily slammed dishes into the sink. After two or three dishes hit the sink, Conrad approached her to try to talk to her. Kim completely ignored him. Jordan started crying. Kim went into Jordan's room and picked her up out of her crib. She and the baby went upstairs to her home office; Conrad followed close behind her.

Kim was sitting at her desk in the office and, again, Conrad got in her face.

"What's wrong with you? Why are you walking around slamming dishes?"

"Get out of my face. You're such a damn liar! You're not interested in sex anymore? Is that why you came home last week with a condom in your pocket?" Kim shot back. She spun around in her chair, turning her back to him – as if to dismiss him.

"Don't turn your back to me. I'm talking and that's disrespectful."

"Shut up and get the hell out of my face!"

Without warning, Conrad turned Kim's chair around and slapped her across her face while she was holding their eight-week-old daughter in her arms. In defense, Kim punched Conrad in his private area and picked up the phone on the fax machine and dialed 911.

Conrad was irate. He snatched Jordan out of Kim's hands and proceeded to smash the fax machine with one hand while holding Jordan in the other. Unfortunately for

Conrad, the call went through and the police dispatcher called the house right back.

Kim had the police come escort Conrad out of the house. She called her parents and told them what happened. They came over to her house and by 3:00 a.m. the next morning, she had pressed domestic violence charges against Conrad.

They were separated for three months. During this time, the court allowed them to seek anger management counseling and they completed an eight-week course. Kim and Conrad both sought the Lord and petitioned the court to throw out the charges.

Upon reviewing the case and hearing from both Kim and Conrad and their desire to try to make their marriage work, the judge threw the domestic violence charges out.

Kim talked with her parents and her prayer partner, but she still wasn't sure that she had made the right decision – staying with Conrad. But Kim wanted to make sure that she gave her marriage her all. Kim wanted Jordan to grow up with her mommy and her daddy. Most of all, Kim wanted to remain true to God and her marriage vows.

SEEKING GOD

Everyone is quick to tell you what the Bible says and how to apply it to your circumstances. We run around telling our stories of misfortune, manipulation, degradation and the like to our girlfriends, mothers, sisters, etc., but we don't tell the one person who can give us divine wisdom and instruction – God. God knows all things. He promises to supply our every need and He promises to never leave us nor forsake us.

When we are in the thick of things, we need to seek God. We are supposed to seek God in **all** things. The Bible says to "Lean on, trust in, *and* be confident in the Lord with all your heart *and* mind and do not rely on your own insight *or* understanding. In all your ways know, recognize, and acknowledge Him, and He will direct *and* make straight *and* plain your paths (Proverbs 3:5-6 AMP).

---

*P*ray about your
circumstances instead
of worrying about them.

When faced with a dilemma, we need to fall on our face and seek the Lord through prayer and supplication, "Do not be anxious about anything, but in everything, by prayer and petition, with thanksgiving, present your requests to God. And the peace of all God, which transcends all understanding, will guard your hearts and your minds in Christ Jesus (Philippians 4:6-7)."

Pray about your circumstances instead of worrying about them. God tells us not to worry because He cares for us and will provide for us, "Therefore I tell you, do not worry about your life, what you will eat or drink; or about your body, what you will wear...Look at the birds of the air...your heavenly father feeds them. Are you much more valuable then they? Who of you by worrying can add a single hour to his life (Matthew 6:25-27)?"

PRAYER

Prayer is communication with God. Effective prayer comes from a heart that places its trust in God. God speaks to us through the Bible and we speak to Him through prayer. Assured by Scripture that God is personal, living, active, all knowing, all wise, and all-powerful, we know that God can hear and answer us. Prayer is a request to a personal Lord who answers, as He knows best.

Praise God that we each have our own intimate relationship with God and that we are able to come to Him and have our requests be made known unto Him. Because Christ died for our sins, we no longer need man to intercede on our behalf by sacrificing sin offerings. Jesus is on the right hand of the Father interceding on our behalf (Romans 8:34).

Therefore, whatever your needs, take them to the Lord, "Let us hold unswervingly to the hope we profess, for he who promised is faithful (Hebrews 10:23)." If we do our part, there is no question that God will fulfill his part of the covenant (2 Timothy 2:11-13).

God will also give us wisdom with regard to how to handle our situations, " If any of you lacks wisdom, he should ask God, who gives generously to all without finding fault, and it will be given to him. But when he asks, he must believe and not doubt, because he who doubts is like a wave of the sea, blown and tossed by the wind (James 1:5-6)."

Once God gives you wisdom, believe Him. Don't go asking your girls, calling your mother, or seeking a second opinion from *anyone*. You must guard what God gives you with diligence. The devil is just waiting to steal your peace and confound your thoughts so that he can keep you bound up.

Seek God and He will give you the answers and guidance that you need, " 'Then you will call upon me and come and pray to me, and I will listen to you. You will seek me and find me when you seek me with all your heart. I will be found by you' declares the Lord... (Jeremiah 29:12-14)"

REFLECTION QUESTIONS

1. What dilemmas are you trusting God to resolve?

2. Why is it a sin to worry?

3. What is prayer?

4. How does God communicate with us?

5. Why is it important to guard the wisdom that God gives you with diligence?

CHAPTER SIX

Thy Will Be Done

Veronica didn't know how much more she could take. She was finding it harder and harder to act like everything was okay. Even though Mike continued to hurt her and blame her for his actions, she didn't know if she could live without him.

He was the only man that she had ever loved. She didn't trust him anymore, but she had given him too much – her youth, her heart, her mind, her body, her soul, and her spirit. Thank God for the Temple of Faith and her mentor, Lori Smith.

Veronica met Lori at the bank. Lori is the Pastor of Finance at Faith Temple and she handles all of the finances for the church. Veronica had been promoted to Banking Center Office Manager and as such, she was responsible for reconciling Faith Temple's bank accounts.

Every Monday Lori would call Veronica to confirm receipt totals for the church's Sunday deposits. Lori would also come in on Thursday afternoon to discuss the mid-week service deposits that were made on Wednesday evenings.

Over the past year, the two women had grown close. At first, Veronica was not sure what it was about Lori that made her feel comfortable. Usually, she did not care much for women. Women either wanted her man or wanted to be all up in her business. As for the women at the bank, they were either jealous or plain nosy.

Tammy and Carmen were the two women closest to Veronica's age at the bank. Veronica tried to be cool with them, but they were always making some type of snide remark.

"Girl, I'm not trying to be all up in your business, but how much money do you make an hour? I mean, how can you afford to drive a Lexus truck?"

One time Veronica overheard the two of them talking about how she dressed.

"That Gucci bag is probably a fake" said Carmen.

"No, it's not" Replied Tammy, "You know her man is a hustler."

Veronica tried to ignore them, but she would be lying if she said that it didn't bother her.

Instead, she tried to befriend the older women at

her job. They were nice, but over time, they tried to act like her mama.

"Veronica, when are you going to get that boy to marry you and do right by you and those kids?" Mrs. Jones asked.

"What does he do for a living?" Miss Nadine chimed in.

"Baby, you got too much going for yourself to be tied down to the likes of him" Ms. Jones said as the two women shook their heads in disgust.

Veronica felt as though she could not win for losing, so she decided to mind her own business and keep to herself while she was at work. For the most part, she was quiet and withdrawn. She came to work everyday, did her job and went home. She never joined the other ladies for lunch and rarely discussed anything other than bank-related business.

That all changed when she met Lori. There was something about Lori that was warm and inviting. She instantly liked Lori. So, the day that Lori asked Veronica if she had a church home, Veronica felt comfortable telling her about how she used to go to church with her grandmother as a little girl.

"My grandmother died when I was eight years old and I never went back to church after her that" Veronica told Lori.

"Oh" Lori replied, and with a big smile on her face she said, "Well, we have a great deal of young people who attend Faith Temple, and we have a great daycare. I think that you and your family would really enjoy my church. So, if you ever want to visit, you can be my guest. We would love to have you!"

Veronica made up an excuse as to why she couldn't visit, but thanked Lori for the invitation.

A couple of weeks later when Lori came in, she noticed that Veronica was upset and asked her if everything was all right. Veronica couldn't believe what happened next. When she opened up her mouth, the truth about her situation came flooding out. Veronica had just hung up the phone because she was tired of arguing with Mike about his life style and their marriage.

Veronica was mentally and physically exhausted. She was 25 years old with three children. She didn't feel like she was going anywhere in life. Veronica took her lunch break and the two women went to a quiet coffee shop where Veronica poured out her hurt and frustration.

She told Lori about her childhood and about Mike. She confessed that at one time in her life, Mike had been her "knight in shining armor." Whenever things weren't going right at home because her mom was tied up at work or stuck on her new boyfriend, Veronica could always count on Mike to be there for her. Mike gave her lunch money, bought her clothes, got her hair done; she counted on him for everything and he took good care of her.

"I loved him and I wanted to spend the rest of my life with him", Veronica said rolling her eyes. "When Little Mike was born, we were both happy. We were just kids ourselves – young and stupid," she said.

Veronica even told Lori about the abuse. "The first

time he slapped me I was in shock. Some guy was trying to talk to me and Mike thought that I had been flirting. I was silly enough to think that his possessiveness and jealousy were signs that he really loved me" she admitted, shamefully.

Veronica had never shared this with anyone. She didn't know how Lori would respond and she worried whether or not this would change how Lori perceived her.

Lori took Veronica's hands in hers and smiled that warm, compassionate smile and said, "Veronica, Jesus loves you. No matter what you've done or have been through, Jesus loves you. All this time, He has been keeping you, and He wants to give you life and give it to you more abundantly. Jesus wants to be in relationship with you. Only the Lord can give you the peace, comfort, and love that you seek. Are you willing to let Him love you?"

Veronica sat perfectly still. Every word that Lori said seared itself into her heart and mind. Hot tears began to trickle silently down her cheeks.

Lori continued, "If you are willing, then together we will pray the prayer of salvation."

Right there, in the middle of the "Petite Coffee Shop", Veronica confessed her sins, accepted Jesus as her Lord and Savior, and, therefore, was saved.

God's Will

God created man in his own image to have

dominion over the earth and to do God's will (Genesis 1: 26). Most importantly, man was created to commune with God. Throughout the Old Testament men continued to allow sin to separate them from God, but God repeatedly intervened to draw man back to himself. Ultimately, He sent Jesus – the Redeemer – to be the absolute sin offering for man. We were not only created to fellowship with God but to glorify Him.

---

*A*s we mature spiritually, we realize that it's not what we desire that matters, but what God desires for us.

When God created us, He also gave us free will – the faculty by which we determine to do or not to do something. Our will is determined by what we desire. We all have desires and preconceived notions about how we think that our lives should turn out. It's human nature. We would be less than truthful if we said that we didn't desire to be successful, wealthy, loved, powerful, etc...

Nevertheless, as we mature spiritually, we realize that it's not what we desire that matters, but what God desires for us. We should approach God each day resolved to do his will, "I desire to do your will, O my God; your law is within my heart (Psalm 40:8)".

The Psalmist, David, was a man after God's own heart because he sought to do the will of God. Certainly,

David was not without sin. He was not perfect and, like us all, he made mistakes. What set David apart was his willingness to repent of his wrongdoing and follow God's leadership. We need to embody the attitude of David and "delight yourself in the Lord and he will give you the desires of your heart (Psalm 37:4)."

Knowing God's Will

The Bible admonishes us, "Therefore do not be foolish, but understand what the Lord's will is (Ephesians 5:17)." Discerning the will of the Lord is not a matter of feeling or emotion, but of mental understanding and applying our minds to scripture. God's plans for us are consistently good, when the plans belong to God, we can be assured that we can expect something great, "I will instruct you and teach you in the way you should go; I will counsel you and watch over you (Psalm 32:8)."

In order to have God's vital instructions we must crucify the flesh and submit our will to His. We must actively pursue God's will by asking him to reveal His will to us:

> ..."Come let us go up to the mountain of the Lord, to the Temple of the God of Israel. There he will teach us his ways, so that we may obey them "... - Isaiah 2:3 NLT

> Oh, that we might know the Lord! Let us press on to know him! Then he will

respond to us... – Hosea 6:3 NLT

If you want to know what God wants you to do – ask him, and he will gladly tell you. He will not resent your asking.
– James 1:5 NLT

Once you have submitted your will to God, then He will be faithful to answer you and give you the desires of your heart, "Do not conform any longer to the pattern of this world, but be transformed by the renewing of your mind. Then you will be able to test and approve what God's will is – his good, pleasing and perfect will (Romans 12:2)."

Knowing God's will for your life will give you increased wisdom, "Your commands make me wiser than my enemies, for your commands are my constant guide...(Psalm 119:96-106)." We already know that the devil comes to kill, steal, and destroy, but thank God that He is faithful to keep us!

If we trust God and rely on Him, the Bible says that "This is the confidence we have in approaching God: that if we ask anything according to his will, he hears us. And if we know that he hears us – whatever we ask – we know that we have what we asked of him. (1 John 5:14-15)."

Rejoice because God intends on getting the glory out of the very situation you're in now, no matter how ugly or difficult. You are an overcomer in Jesus name!

And the very thing that the devil tried to use to kill you, God is going to use to demonstrate his majesty! You are blessed because not only are you coming out of the valley, but you're also going to bring other women out with you. Hallelujah!

<u>REFLECTION QUESTIONS</u>

1. How does sin separate us from God?

2. How was David a man after God's own heart?

3. What must we do to know God's will for our life?

4. How do we benefit from knowing God's will for our life?

Part III

Finding the Courage to Leave

"Be strong and courageous. Do not be afraid or terrified because of them, for the Lord your God goes with you; he will never leave you nor forsake you"

Deuteronomy 31:6

CHAPTER SEVEN

Understanding the Consequences

For months now, Gloria had been finding comfort in food. Eating made her feel better. Food was her friend. She spent a lot of time alone and most of that time she spent eating. She had even slacked off at church. She barely made it to church on Sunday and, of course, David never joined church after all. She was so happy to finally get a man and now her whole world focused around David.

That all changed the day that she received an irate phone call from Stacey Cox. Stacey Cox was a member of her church and the mother of Kendra Cox. Kendra was eighteen years old and she had sung in the church choir most of her life. Gloria introduced David to Kendra's mother, Stacey, and he began working on the production for Kendra's debut solo project a few months later.

"Gloria, I need to talk to you." Stacey's voice shook with anger.

"What's going on?" Gloria asked.

"It's Kendra. I think that she and David have something going on!"

"What!" Gloria couldn't believe what she was hearing. She suddenly felt sick to her stomach.

"Last night, Kendra's cell phone was chiming on the kitchen counter. When I picked it up I noticed that she had a new text message from David. I thought that he might be text messaging her about the album or studio time, so I read it. It read "Last night was great, baby. You made me feel so good; I just can't stop thinking about you!"

"Maybe he was talking about her singing." Gloria knew that wasn't what he was talking about, but she was scrambling to come up with an acceptable explanation that would make her and Stacey feel better.

"I asked her." Stacey said pointedly.

Gloria was afraid to hear the answer.

"And she told me that she loves him."

_____

David had a rude awakening when he came home that night. All of his bags were packed and sitting by the front door.

"What the hell is this Gloria; why are my bags

packed?" He screamed.

"So now you're screwing around with Kendra?" Gloria said coldly.

"What the hell are you talking about? Where did you get that nonsense? You're tripping. Go put my bags up."

"Oh, it's nonsense? Is that why your little girlfriend confessed it all to her mother? Let me see, what did the text message say, 'Last night was great, baby. You made me feel so good; I just can't stop thinking about you!'"

"O.k. O.k. Listen, Glo'. It was one time, baby. She don't mean nothing to me." David pleaded.

"Get your stuff and get out!" Gloria yelled.

"What was I supposed to do. Kendra was coming into the studio throwing herself at me? I asked you to lose weight. I told you that I wasn't attracted to you with the weight!"

"You were supposed to be a man who loves his wife, who is faithful to his wife – who has some integrity and self-control!"

"But this wouldn't have happened if you would have done what I asked you to do." David whined.

"Get out!", yelled Gloria.

Gloria knew that everything in her life was about to change. The Bible says that everything done in the dark will come to light (1 Corinthians 4:5). If she decided to end her marriage, officially, her financial and spiritual situation will be precarious, at best.

Spiritual Consequences

There are consequences, good and bad, for every decision that we make. The Bible says that, " How much better to get wisdom than gold, to choose understanding rather than silver (Proverbs 16:16)!" In other words, God does not prevent us from acting foolishly, he only reminds us of the consequences. That's why it is very important that we go to the Lord in prayer, before we make a decision that will impact our lives and our walk with God.

We have already discussed God's intention for marriage in the previous chapters, but let me reiterate that marriage is a covenant that is not to be entered into lightly. Rather, it is a holy condition founded by God and is not to be dissolved, solely, at the will of man. Consequently, when one is considering ending their marriage it is a grave decision that has far reaching ramifications.

On the other hand, if you are still in an abusive relationship and you continue to subject yourself to that abuse, you must take into account how that sinful behavior is affecting others (i.e. children , family, etc.). Consider the story of Jonah:

> So they asked him, "Tell us, who is responsible for making all this trouble for us? What do you do? Where do you come from? What is your country? From what people arc you?" He

answered, "I am a Hebrew and I worship the Lord, the God of heaven, who made the sea and the land." This terrified them and they asked, "What have you done?" (They knew that he was running away from the Lord, because he had already told them so) (Jonah 1:8-10).

Our sinful actions affect more people than just ourselves. Beware of the temptation to rationalize your sins or someone else's sins by saying that you're not hurting anyone else but yourself.

But your iniquities have separated you from your God; your sins have hidden his face from you, so that he will not hear. For your hands are stained with blood, and your fingers with guilt. Your lips have spoken lies, and your tongue mutters wicked things. No one calls for justice; no one pleads his case with integrity. They rely on empty arguments and speak lies; they conceive trouble and give birth to evil (Isaiah 59:2-4).

Sin equates to lawlessness (1 John 3:4) or transgression of God's will, either by omitting to do what God's law requires or by doing what it forbids. The transgression can occur in thought (1 John 3:15), word (Matthew 5:22), or deed (Romans 1:32). Sin is nothing less than rebellion.

The wages of sin is death (Romans 6:23). Because "all have sinned and fall short of the glory of God" (Romans 3:23), all men are spiritually dead – separated from God who is the Source of spiritual life. Sin makes a person hate the light and despise truth; it causes one to break God's laws and become insensitive to holy things. ***Everyone who has not been redeemed by Christ is spiritually dead*** (Luke 15:32, Ephesians 2:1-3, Colossians 2:13, EMPHASIS ADDED).

Natural Consequences

Women who are in abusive relationships find it very difficult to leave. The nature of domestic violence encourages conditions that keep a woman economically dependent and socially isolated. Women in these circumstances have to overcome many barriers when leaving an abusive relationship.

Lack of Financial Resources / No Where to Go

A person being victimized by domestic violence may not have access to money. In many cases, she is forbidden to work and the abuser has total control of the finances. For women who don't have the financial resources to care for and support themselves and their children, the thought of leaving seems impossible.

Because isolation is a part of abuse, the person being victimized may not have supportive friends or family to turn to, or if there is support, it may not be safe to go there. Thus, financial constraints are significant barriers for victims attempting to leave.

Threats

When a woman leaves an abusive relationship the risk of homicide increases. Physical violence, threats and intimidation are very real concerns. Additionally, they fear that if the abuser finds them that they and/or their children will be in danger. Some women fear the unknown – the ramifications of life without the abuser.

Social and Religious Stigmas

Many victims are concerned about what their neighbors and members of their faith community will think if they leave or report the abuse. Stigmas regarding domestic violence, divorce and single parenthood make it difficult for victims to reach out for help.

In some cases, the Bible has been used, out of context, to substantiate abuse and the control of a husband over his wife. Women fear being cast out of their religious community if she divorces her husband due to domestic violence.

Let's Stay Together

A victim may minimize the seriousness of the abuse, deny that it occurs, or except blame for the abusive behavior in order to keep her family in tact. Women don't want to see their family torn apart at their children's expense, especially when the children are not being physically abused.

The devil is a liar! If God has released you from your abusive relationship and you can rest assured that he will protect you and keep you during your time of transition. If you have children, then you are accountable for their welfare.

Children are a gift from God, and we are accountable for what we teach them by word and deed, "Only be careful, and watch yourselves closely so that you do not forget the things that your eyes have seen or let them slip from your heart as long as you live. Teach them to your children and to their children after them (Deuteronomy 4:9)."

REFLECTION QUESTIONS

1. Why is it important to go to the Lord in prayer before we make a decision?

2. If you are in an abusive relationship and you continue to subject yourself to that abuse how has that behavior affected others?

3. In what ways can you relate to the story of Jonah?

4. How have you rationalized your sins or someone else's sins by saying that you're not hurting anyone else but yourself?

5. If applicable, what barriers would you need to overcome in order to leave the abusive relationship?

CHAPTER EIGHT

<u>Making the Decision</u>

Kim had lost track of the number of times that a well-meaning sister in Christ had told her that "God hates divorce!" Kim knew what the Word said. She knew that marriage is the outward manifestation of how Christ loves the church. Over and over in her mind she heard, "What God has put together, let no man put asunder". For years, she struggled in her marriage, enduring physical and mental abuse, infidelity, countless separations, and poor decision-making, which led to the near destruction of herself.

Frankly, she was tired of the barrage of opinions

and advice all given under the guise of "Godly counsel." No longer would she let herself be swayed by the opinions, thoughts, and suggestions of others. No longer would she allow herself to be led, solely, by the wisdom of others. She wanted to know what God had to say. She had made the costly mistake of entering into her marriage without consulting God. She would not continue one way or the other, without His leading...

"Lord, forgive me...I need to be released from my marriage", Kim wrote in her journal.

———

It was the day after Christmas, and everything had been great, considering. Conrad was not a big fan of Kim's family, especially her mother. Kim's brother and his family came for the holidays and she was really enjoying their visit.

Prior to the holiday, Kim and Conrad had worked out a deal. Kim's family planned to open up Christmas gifts together on Christmas morning so that everyone could enjoy the kids' reaction to what Santa Claus had left them. Knowing that Conrad would not be comfortable and fearing the worst, Kim agreed to a compromise with Conrad regarding the holiday festivities.

"You know that I don't like your parents. Why can't we just celebrate Christmas by ourselves at our own home?"

Although Conrad had agreed weeks earlier to the holiday arrangements, now two days before Christmas, he had changed his mind.

"You agreed to this two weeks ago." Kim said ,annoyed.

Kim was so tired of going back and forth with Conrad over this.

"All right, what do you want to do? I have already told my parents that we would open our gifts at their house with everyone else. What do you expect me to tell them two days before Christmas?"

"Fine. I shouldn't expect for you to care about my feelings anyway."

Here we go, Kim thought. "Where do you want to spend Christmas?"

"I mean, I can go anywhere. All of my boy's are having something. Can I go over Mark's?"

"Fine, Conrad. As long as you open up Christmas gifts with my family, without having an attitude, then I don't have a problem with you going over Mark's house."

Kim was willing to agree to anything to ensure that there would not be any drama.

"What about the day after Christmas?" She asked nervously.

Kim was afraid that Conrad would try to back out of the family dinner that they were supposed to host after her family attended church service with them.

"Do they have to come back here? I don't want your family in our house."

Kim felt herself beginning to boil over. Everything that they had discussed and Conrad had agreed to earlier was going out the window. Kim tried to calm down by *reminding herself not to give place to the devil.*

"I mean, they can come, but do I have to be here?"

Again, Kim tried to keep her voice calm and her body language in check, "What do you mean, do you have to be here? Of course you do. How would it look if you weren't here? Come on now, we talked about his already and you gave me your word. It's one weekend out of your life."

"Okay, relax." Conrad said smiling. "I'll be here. I guess I should be happy that my baby understood my feelings and agreed to let me hang out with my boys."

Kim was excited about the holidays. This was the first Christmas since her marriage that she could afford to get her husband, her daughter, and her two nephews Christmas gifts.

Christmas was nice, and as promised, when Conrad got up to go, Kim made his excuses and kissed him goodbye. She and Jordan stayed there until Conrad came to pick them up later that night. Kim's family attended church the next morning, and Kim was really feeling good about their visit to her church.

After the service, Kim's family was going out to breakfast and she was going to join them.

"I don't want to go." Conrad said.

"You're not hungry?"

"I told you that I'm not feeling your parents."

"So you don't care if Jordan and I go?"

"No, have a good time. I'm going to stay here with Pastor. I'll eat with him."

Moments later, Conrad came running up to Kim as

she walked out the door.

"I'm going." He said annoyed.

"What happened to staying with Pastor?"

"I'm hungry. I want to eat, too."

"Are you going to be able to sit there and be civil?" Kim asked concerned.

"I don't have to talk to eat."

This infuriated Kim. She couldn't understand how someone could profess to dislike people, not want them in his house, but have no problem using them for favors, money, support, and anything else that he needed.

On the way to the restaurant, Conrad continued to press the matter.

"Why can't you understand where I'm coming from?"

"I did. That's why when you wanted to go over your boy's house, I compromised."

"As usual, you get your way. Don't worry about it, Kim, I'm going. I'm always the one who has to give in. I'll always lose out to your parents."

"And what is that supposed to mean?"

"It means that you love them more than you love me!" Conrad's bottom lip trembled as he yelled.

"Now, that's just ridiculous. The two don't even compare. It's like comparing apples to oranges. I'm tired of going back and forth with you regarding my parents. At this point, I don't even have an appetite. I'm going home." Kim pulled out her cell phone and called her mother.

"Mom, I'm tired. We're just going to go home. I'll

catch up with you guys later. Okay? Bye."

"Why did you do that? I'm hungry. What am I supposed to do now?" Conrad said.

"I'll cook at home."

"I don't want the food that we have at home. So now I have to suffer? I can't go out to eat? I want to go get something to eat. Can I take your car?" Conrad did not have a car when she met him. And when Kim's parents gave him their car, he traded it in for another car that, in the end, never left the car lot due to engine troubles.

"No."

"What am I supposed to do?"

"The same thing that you always do. Call one of your boys to come and get you."

Kim pulled up in their driveway, took Jordan out of her car seat and went into the house. She had a feeling that Conrad would try to take her car keys so that he could take the car, so she put them in her jean pocket as she walked into the house.

Kim hung her coat up in the front closet and sat her purse on the living room sofa. As she pulled the bacon and eggs out of the refrigerator, she saw Conrad going through her coat pockets.

"My car keys aren't in there, Conrad."

Conrad sighed as put her coat back and then walked over to the sofa where Kim's purse sat. He picked it up and began going through it. He tossed her belongings, one by one, out onto the sofa.

"My keys aren't in there, either." Kim stated emotionless.

With that said, he threw her purse down and turned towards her. Kim dropped the keys into the crotch of her panties just as Conrad lunged at her. He grabbed her forcefully from behind as he frantically tried to retrieve the keys. Jordan just looked on, terrified.

"Get off of me! Stop it! Look at Jordan! Look at what you're doing in front of her!" Kim screamed.

Conrad just kept on pushing and shoving Kim. Kim called out to Jordan as she began to cry. She couldn't believe that he was attacking her, again, in front of their two-year old daughter. Jordan ran to her mother and held on to Kim's leg. Jordan began crying, too. She was horrified. She kept yelling for her daddy to stop hurting her mommy.

Conrad was unmoved by his daughter's pleas. He wrestled Kim down to the ground and proceeded to pull the legs on Kim's jean to get to the keys she had placed in the crotch of her panties. Kim didn't want to continue fighting him in the presence of their daughter. She pulled the keys out of her crotch.

"If you take my car, I'm going to call the police and report it stolen."

Conrad snatched the keys out of her hands and ran out of the house. He peeled out of the driveway as Kim dialed 911 with Jordan still clutching her leg. Kim filed a police report and contacted their pastor. Pastor Benson was able to talk Conrad into returning the car so that Kim wouldn't have to file grand theft auto charges.

Kim reconciled within herself that she would never be in this position again. Despite the turmoil that her life *had been in up to this point, deep within her spirit, she had a quiet peace that told her that everything would be all right. She sensed that her marriage was over and that God had finally released her.*

Making the Right Choice

If you are contemplating ending your marriage, God will give you the wisdom to make the right decision. Knowing the Scriptures and gleaming their wisdom gives us more options in our decision making and provides us with the discernment we need to make healthy choices. The correct decision is the one that is consistent with the principles of truth found in God's Word.

The Bible tells us that as long as we seek God's will He will direct our paths (Proverbs 3:6). We must make the choice that will please God. In the instance where there are several options that are consistent with the Word of God, then instead of focusing on the decision, we must trust God to help us make the most of the path that we choose.

> Show me your ways, O Lord,
> teach me your paths; guide me
> in your truth and teach me, for
> you are God my Savior, and
> my hope is in you all day long
> (Psalm 25:4-5).

You will know that you have made the right decision when you have the peace of God. Peace refers to the inner tranquility and poise of the Christian whose trust is in God. When we seek God and obey His commands the Bible says that "...the God of peace (of untroubled, undisturbed well-being) will be with you (Philippians 4:9 AMP)."

Fasting

You should always consider fasting when you are earnestly seeking God's guidance and direction. Biblical fasting is going without food or drink, voluntarily, for the purposes of setting oneself apart for God's use, "Then Esther sent this reply to Mordecai: 'Go, gather together all the Jews who are in Susa, and fast for me. Do not eat or drink for three days, night or day' (Esther 4:15-16)."

Fasting proves to God that we are concerned about the things of God. During a fast, we humble ourselves by abstaining from food and focusing on glorifying God, enhancing our spirit and going deeper in our prayer life.

> "Why have we fasted," they say,
> "and you have not seen it? Why
> have we humbled ourselves,
> and you have not noticed?'...
> 'Yet on the day of your fasting,
> you do as you please...Your
> fasting ends in quarreling and
> strife, and in striking each
> other with wicked fists. You

> cannot fast as you do today
> and expect your voice to be
> heard on high...Is not this the
> kind of fasting I have chosen:
> to loose the chains of injustice
> and untie the cords of the yoke,
> to set the oppressed free and
> break every yoke? (Isaiah 58:3-
> 6)."

We fast to demonstrate that we are seeking God "with all of our heart." It also allows us to be able to hear from God more clearly by putting things into proper perspective. A fast always includes prayer and studying God's Word.

> Declare a holy fast; call a sacred
> assembly. Summon the elders
> and all who live in the land
> to the house of the Lord your
> God, and cry out to the Lord
> (Joel 1:14).

Fasting helps us to find God's will. We must put God first in order for him to direct our steps. This means denying to self so that we can focus our attention on Him. We find an example of fasting for direction in 2 Chronicles 20:1-30. Three nations were coming against Judah to destroy them. King Jehoshaphat, the king of Judah, proclaimed a fast for the whole nation and they asked the Lord what they should do. God heard their prayer and honored their fast and gave the people prophetic direction through one of the choir members – God told them what to do.

Acts 13:2 is yet another example of direction being given by God during a fast. The leaders of the church of Antioch worshipped and fasted and the Holy Spirit told the church leaders to choose Paul and Barnabas from among their group to spread the gospel among the Gentiles.

When we take our eyes off the things of this world, we can look to God, "Then your light shall break forth like the morning, your healing shall spring forth speedily, and your righteousness shall go before you; the glory of the Lord shall be your rear guard. Then you shall call, and the Lord will answer; you shall cry, and He will say, 'Here I am' (Isaiah 58:8-9)."

REFLECTION QUESTIONS

1. In what ways are you seeking God's wisdom to help you make healthy choices?

2. What scriptures have you used or are you using?

3. How have you incorporated fasting into your decision making process?

4. How have you incorporated prayer into your fast?

5. What did God reveal to you during your fast?

CHAPTER NINE

Next Steps

Veronica fumbled nervously as she threw the kid's clothing into a garbage bag. She knew that she had to get as much as she could, as quickly as she could, without getting caught. She worked frantically as she tried to remember to get all of the essentials...

Veronica had really been growing in the Lord since she joined Faith Temple. She faithfully attended church each Sunday and had even begun going to Bible study on Wednesdays. Her kids liked the church, too.

She was especially impressed with how the young

men took to and mentored little Mike. Little Mike was only seven years old, but she was afraid of the example that Mike was setting for him. She hated for him to spend time with his father. Mike and his friends didn't think that anything was wrong with them smoking and drinking around him. Needless to say, she was extremely happy that at Faith Temple Little Mike had godly men with which to look up to and emulate.

The girls were also growing spiritually. They enjoyed Sunday school and expressed an interest in getting baptized. Veronica was really trying to live holy. She had stopped drinking and she was trying very hard to stop cursing.

"Damn it, drive!" Veronica yelled as she hit her horn to let the driver in front of her know that the light had changed a good two minutes ago.

"Mommy, you're not supposed to use bad language. Sister Linda says that it makes God sad when we use bad language." Madison is five years old going on twenty-five. Madison thought that she was Kim's mother instead of it being the other way around.

"I know, honey. Mommy is sorry. I hate being late to Bible study, but that's no excuse to use bad language. Mommy will tell God sorry, too, so that He can forgive me. That's called repentance."

"Re-pent-ance." Madison repeated.

"Yes. It is when we tell God that we're sorry for doing something that He told us not to do, and we promise not to do it again."

"Oh." Madison replied. She loved to talk about and

learn about the Bible. Madison knew that Jesus loved her and died for her sins. She was like a little sponge – anything that she was told about the Bible – she retained. Veronica was amazed at the number of scriptures that Madison had already memorized.

McKenzie is the quiet one. She is a Mama's girl. She is two years old and enjoys being the baby. The entire family dotes on her. McKenzie really enjoys attending the daycare at the church. During service, the nursery workers read the children Bible stories, they color and McKenzie plays with the other children. Both girls are members of the Jr. Faith Praise Team. They dance every fourth Sunday.

Veronica had worked from 9:00 a.m. to 6:00 p.m. today. She picked the kids up from aftercare and daycare in just enough time to get to Bible study. Bible study starts at 7:00 p.m. and Veronica didn't like getting there late. She took little snacks and coloring books to keep the girls occupied while she and Little Mike enjoyed the mid-week service.

At first, Mike didn't have a problem with Veronica attending Faith Temple. Although that changed when she stopped drinking and wanting to party.

"What, you think you too good to kick it? You a 'goody-two-shoes' or something?" He said laughing.

"No. I just don't want to drink anymore."

"Ain't nothing wrong with having some fun, baby."

"I know."

"You acting like you in a cult or something."

"No, I'm not Mike. I'm just trying to live holy. I want

to be right before God. Why don't you come to church with us?"

"Hell naw! I don't want to go to no church. I know that God loves me. I don't need a bunch of phony hypocrites judging the way that I live."

"It's not like that. They don't judge you. They just teach you about the Bible and what God expects of us as Christians."

"Nope. I'm straight."

Veronica just left it alone. She had tried on several occasions to get Mike to go to church with her and the kids, but he always turned her down. Eventually, she stopped asking him to go. Over time, he became more and more belligerent about her attending church.

"You going to church again?" Mike asked snidely.

"They're having a youth program at the church today."

"It seems like they're always having something at that damn church. If you put in as much time around here as you do down there, then maybe I could get a home cooked meal or the house would be cleaned. Did you know that I had to go out and buy me some more underwear because I don't have anymore clean ones? When is the last time that you washed some clothes?"

"I'm going to clean the house and wash the clothes this weekend." Veronica responded. She felt like he was trying to get something started, but she wasn't going to give the devil place.

"I'm hungry. What about dinner?"

"Can you pick something up, tonight?" She asked

hoping that he would agree.

"I'm tired of eating out. I want some home cooking. I tell you what; once you have things together here then you can go to church."

"What?" Veronica responded incredulously.

"Look, me and my kids come before all that other bullshit. You need to take care of home. Until you do, then you can forget about that stupid church. I don't want to hear anything else about it." Mike gave her the look that dared her to say anything other than o.k.

Veronica took her coat off and walked into the kitchen to pull some steaks out of the freezer for dinner. Little Mike came into the kitchen with his coat on wondering when they were going to leave for church.

"Ma, hurry up. We're going to be late."

Mike walked into the kitchen.

"I'm going out, I'll be back in a couple of hours." Mike said as he walked out of the back door of the house.

"Ma, what about church?" Little Mike was anxious to get there. He had written a poem that he was going to recite during the youth program.

"We're not going to be able to go tonight. Daddy wants us to stay home and have dinner with him."

"But Ma, I'm supposed to be doing my poem. Besides, Daddy just said that he won't be back for a couple of hours." Little Mike pleaded with his mother.

Veronica hated to disappoint the kids. Truthfully, she was excited that Little Mike had agreed to take part in the youth program because she didn't think that he would even be interested. She was tired of Mike controlling everything by telling her what she could and could not do.

"O.k. Go tell your sisters to hurry up so that we won't be late."

The youth program was wonderful! The Jr. Faith Praise Team danced and the girls did great. Little Mike's poem was beautiful – it talked about how God loves and watches over us. Veronica was beaming with pride. She thanked and praised God for the things that He was doing in her and in her children.

She was so full of the joy of the Lord that she completely forgot about Mike. When she walked into the house, he was sitting on the couch. He hollered at the kids to take off their coats, go to their rooms and go to bed. Veronica knew that he had been drinking by the way his words slurred. She kissed each of the kids on their heads and told them to do as their father told them.

By the time the kids had reached their rooms, Mike was in her face!

"So you went anyway!" He said, as he back handed her across her face.

Veronica braced herself for the next blow. She knew that there was nothing that she could say or do to save herself. She used to cry and beg for him to stop but now, she withdrew somewhere deep inside herself. She had defied him and there would be hell to pay. Moments later, she struggled to her feet. Mike had grown tired of beating her. He went into their bedroom and passed out across the bed.

Veronica went into the bathroom to wash the blood off her face. As she placed a wet towel up to her bruised and bleeding mouth, she caught a glimpse of herself in the mirror. Her eye was blacken and her face was swollen. Something inside of her snapped. The empty void that had been numb for so long began to writhe with pain. Deep wrenching sobs that sounded like they were being torn from her very soul resonated from deep within her body.

Veronica went into the bedroom and looked at Mike passed out across the bed.

"Mike, I'm sorry. Mike, are you up? Did you hear me?"

Mike didn't move. His mouth was wide open. Drool trickled out of the side of his mouth. It was if he was in an alcohol induced coma.

Veronica went into the kitchen and got several garbage bags out of the cabinet. She filled up as many garbage bags as she could with her and her kids' clothes. She grabbed all of their social security cards, birth certificates, and important papers. She went through Mike's jean pockets and took all of the cash that he had ($765). She put all of the garbage bags into her car and then got her children up one-by-one and put them in the car.

She called Lori as soon as she got into her car. It was 3:00 a.m. and she didn't know where to go.

"I'm sorry to call you so late. I've left Mike...I took my kids and I left. I don't want to die; I want to live and I need your help." Veronica could barely get the words out *because she was crying so hard.*

"Hush now. The light is on and my door is open. You and your kids are more than welcome to stay here. God has been waiting and so have I. Come on. Everything is going to be just fine."

Veronica could feel God's love envelope her. She suddenly felt completely at peace. She dried her face and drove toward Lori's house.

"Thank you, Lord." Veronica whispered.

Have Faith

When you trust God and avail yourself to Him through prayer, He promises to answer you, "He answered their prayers, because they trusted in him (1 Chronicles 5:20)." Once God answers your prayers and tells you what to do, the only thing left to do is to follow His direction.

Believing that God will fulfill his promise to you by doing what He said He would do, requires faith.

> Now faith is being sure of what
> we hope for and certain of what
> we do not see...By faith we
> understand that the universe
> was formed at God's command,
> so that what is seen was not
> made out of what was visible...
> By faith Enoch was taken from
> this life, so that he did not
> experience death; he could not

be found, because God had
taken him away. For before he
was taken, he was commended
as one who pleased God. And
without faith it is impossible
to please God, because anyone
who comes to him must believe
that he exists and that he
rewards those who earnestly
seek him (Hebrews 11:1-6).

Look beyond your natural circumstances and
know that God is in control, "Don't be afraid, for I am
with you. Don't be dismayed, for I am your God. I will
strengthen you. I will help you. I will hold you with
my victorious right hand (Isaiah 41:10)." Fear is not of
God. It is a trick of the enemy designed to keep us from
receiving the blessings that God has for us. The devil
wants us to be so afraid that we will not obey God and
as a result, forfeit our blessing(s) due to disobedience.

...[God said to Moses,] "because
you did not trust me enough...
you will not lead them into the
land... (Numbers 20:1-13)".

Don't try to do this on your own, instead trust
God and walk in what He tells you to do, "In his heart
a man plans his course, but the Lord determines his
steps (Proverbs 16:9)."

Plan Ahead

If you are a victim of domestic violence, it is critical that you have a safety plan. When physical, emotional, or sexual violence has occurred once in a relationship, it is likely to happen again. Use what you know about the abuser to plan ahead by creating a plan to protect yourself and your children.

If You are Still in an Abusive Relationship:

- Teach your children how to dial 9-1-1.

- Tell trusted friends, family members, and neighbors what's going on.

- Find a safe place to go that the abuser doesn't know about.

- Prepare a bag of clothing, medications, and essentials for yourself and your children in the event that you have to leave suddenly. Hide it where you can get to it quickly.

- Make several copies of important papers and give a set to a family member or close friend

- Create a checklist
    - identification
    - birth certificates for you and your children
    - social security cards
    - money, bank books, credit cards
    - keys – house/car/office

- pets
- insurance papers
- children's favorite toys, blankets
- address book

❧ If it's an emergency and you have to leave the house quickly, DO NOT stop to collect your things.

❧ During an incident of abuse or violence, get out if you can or call 9-1-1. Stay away from the kitchen, bathroom, garage, or other potentially dangerous rooms.

After You are No Longer in an Abusive Relationship

❧ Change your phone number

❧ Change your locks if the abuser leaves. Install security doors, a security system and/or an outside lighting system

❧ Notify your neighbors that your partner no longer lives with you and ask them to call the police if they notice something suspicious

❧ Notify your daycare. Give them the updated name of individuals who have permission to pick your children up.

❧ Screen your calls.

❧ Avoid staying home alone.

❧ Vary your routine by using different stores, banks, etc.

❧ Tell someone about your situation at your place of employment that you trust.

❧ Get a protection order for you and your children and keep a copy with you at all times. Give a copy to the police, your children's caregiver and/or school(s), and your supervisor at work.

❧ Join a support group that will help encourage you when you feel discouraged.

REFLECTION QUESTIONS

1. What promises has God made you that require increased faith in order for you to receive them?

2. How has fear stopped you from obeying God?

3. Why is it important to have a safety plan?

4. Create a Safety plan.

PART IV
LEARNING TO FORGIVE

*A [self-confident] fool utters all his anger, but
a wise man holds it back and stills it.*
Proverbs 29:11 (AMP)

CHAPTER TEN

<u>Be Angry & Sin Not</u>

Kim was seething with anger. Conrad was still preaching at Zion Hill. Not only was he preaching, but even worse, using the pulpit as a vehicle to tell "his side" of why their marriage had failed.

Kim's heart raced. "What do the members of the church think?" She wondered.

It angered her to know that he was still lying and deceiving people at her and their daughter's expense.

Kim's stylist, Tracey, is also a minister at Zion Hill Baptist Church and although Kim thought it best to cut all ties to the church, she could not imagine leaving Tracy. Since Kim would not leave Tracey, she decided to lay down the ground rules at her first appointment following *her separation from Conrad.*

As soon as she sat in Tracey's chair, Kim said, "look, I'm getting a divorce and I don't want to talk about my marriage or talk about Conrad."

At first, Tracey was really cool and she respected Kim's wishes. However, after the initial shock wore off, Tracey could not resist bringing Conrad up at every opportunity. Perhaps Tracey thought that she was helping when, in fact, she was only making matters worse.

"Girl, I know that you're not interested in talking about Conrad, but he preached at church this past Sunday, and Kevin said that it sounded like he was making a confession." Tracey said laughing.

Kim rolled her eyes into the back of her head. She had told Tracey more than once that she didn't want to discuss Conrad nor the details of their separation.

"I don't care." Kim said stoically.

Tracey kept right on talking like Kim hadn't said a word.

"Yeah girl, he said that Conrad was saying 'Y'all know that I am having problems in my marriage. Don't talk about the preacher. Pray for me.'"

"Tracey, for the last time I DON'T CARE." Kim almost yelled the words out. She was so annoyed with Tracey for continuing to bring him up. Kim was more annoyed, however, with the fact that he was still being allowed to preach. Especially since their pastor was well aware of the circumstances surrounding their separation.

Kim and Conrad had been separated for months.

Since Conrad was an associate Pastor at Zion Hill Baptist Church, it was pretty clear that she would need to find a new church home. Conrad and Kim had been separated before and when they reconciled, they praised God and openly shared their testimony with the rest of the congregation.

Therefore, there were other couples in the church whose marriages were strengthened and salvaged through Conrad and Kim's testimony. Conrad and Kim had only been members of the church for a year and a half and of course no one, besides their pastor, knew about the domestic violence.

Now that Kim had officially filed for divorce, she had found some peace and had started to put the past behind her. Instead of feeling defeated by her circumstances, she rejoiced in the peace and hope that the Lord had given her regarding her future.

On occasion, one of the mother's of the church, Mother Cook, would call her to see how she and Jordan were getting along.

"How you doing, baby?" Mother Cook's voice was filled with love and concern.

"I'm really good. Jordan and I are doing quite well. We have been visiting churches and spending time in the Lord's presence."

"I'm still praying for you. God has been showing me things and I have just been praying. You and Conrad are going to be all right."

"Yes, I'm going to be fine. As for the marriage it's over." Kim felt pangs of anger beginning to burn in her *belly.*

"*You know the Lord hates divorce, what about your joint ministry?*" *Mother Cook said.*

"*I know that God hates divorce, but I also know that God loves me and that he would not want me to be in a situation where I was being abused. Nor would God want me to put my daughter in an abusive situation where she grows up thinking that God condones a man putting his hands on a woman, or that she is supposed to submit to that kind of treatment. As far as Conrad's ministry is concerned, that's between him and God.*" *Kim's voice shook with anger. Every time she thought about how Conrad had cheated on her, lied to her, taken advantage of her, and abused her mentally and physically, she became enraged. Her emotions were boiling over, and she couldn't stop her feelings from rising up and flowing out of her mouth.*

"*Everybody is running around after Conrad – praying for his deliverance. What about me and Jordan? He's done nothing for my baby since he's been gone. Oh, yeah he sent her two "Thinking of You" greeting cards. Am I supposed to pay daycare, buy her diapers, food, or clothes with that? He's a liar! He can continue to manipulate and deceive you all, but I'm done!*" *Kim stewed silently as she pondered ways to uncover Conrad as the lying fraud that she knew him to be. She wanted him to lose everything near and dear to him; she wanted him to suffer the way that she had suffered throughout their marriage.*

Mother Cook was silent for a moment. Then, as

even toned as before, she said to Kim, "Baby, I know that you've been done wrong. I know that he hurt you. The Lord has shown me things. Somebody's got to pay for all the wrong that was done to you, but vengeance is mine saith the Lord. You have to pray for your enemies, by doing so you heap coals of fire on their head. That's what the Bible says."

Kim knew what the Bible said. She knew that someway, somehow she had to get past these feelings of hurt and anger. She knew that, ultimately, she was only harming herself and not Conrad when she continued to give in to these feelings of anger.

"Thank you, Mother. I know that you're right. I just don't know how to get past these feelings. My life has been turned upside down since I married him and despite his lack of repentance, things keep right on going for him." Kim said sadly.

"Just trust God, baby. He'll take away the hurt. Let God heal you. Until you are healed, you're no good to yourself or that little girl."

Anger – Spiritual Suicide

Anger is a very dangerous emotion by virtue of the fact that it can blind us to what is good and right. Anger makes us susceptible to do or say things that we will regret because it produces ungodliness and evil motives within us (James 1:19-20).

...The Lord looked with favor
on Abel and his offering, but

on Cain and his offering he
did not look with favor. So
Cain was very angry, and his
face was downcast...And while
they were out in the field, Cain
attacked his brother Abel and
killed him (Genesis 4:4-8).

Even though it's difficult, do not give into anger
and/or encourage it. When we remain angry, we stymie
our spiritual growth and progress. It's all right to be
angry, but it's not all right to remain angry.

"In your anger do not sin": Do
not let the sun go down while
you are still angry, and do
not give the devil a foothold
(Ephesians 4:26-27).

Guard Your Heart

Too many times, we have allowed our emotions to
dictate our perception of the circumstance. The phrase,
"I feel..." has determined many of our "next steps." We
must be careful to not be ruled by our emotions because
it is written that:

The heart is deceitful above all
things, and it is exceedingly
perverse and corrupt and
severely, mortally sick! Who can

know it [perceive, understand,
be acquainted with his own
heart and mind]? (Jeremiah
17:9, AMP)

So we must guard our hearts with all diligence. Don't give the enemy place. Take your heart – the source of your thoughts, feelings and actions – and give it to the Lord, "May the words of my mouth and the meditations of my heart be pleasing in your sight, O Lord, my Rock and my Redeemer (Psalm 19:14)."

Give your opinions and frustrations to God, rather than speak your mind and say or do something that you'll not only regret, but something that you'll have to repent for later! As always, you can depend on God to mend your broken heart, take your anger away, and be your avenger.

"Have I not kept this in reserve
and sealed in my vaults? It is
mine to avenge; I will repay.
In due time their foot will slip;
their day of disaster is near and
their doom rushes upon them
(Deuteronomy 32:34-35)."

Only God, who is completely just, can judge all of the grievances committed against you and make them right.

Bless those who persecute you; bless and do not curse...Do not repay anyone evil for evil. Be careful to do what is right in the eyes of everybody. If it is possible, as far as it depends on you, live at peace with everyone. Do not take revenge, my friends, but leave room for God's wrath...Do not be overcome by evil, but overcome evil with good (Romans 12:14-21).

As Christians, we are called to see the good in everyone, for we are all created in the image of God. As such, we should strive to live peaceably. God understands that peace is not always in our control; But if free from vengeance, we can give ourselves to mercy and acts of kindness. In doing so, we please God and inspire others to "...Hate what is evil; [and] cling to what is good (Romans 12:9)."

REFLECTION QUESTIONS

1. Why is anger a dangerous emotion?

2. What consequences have you faced as a result of acting out of anger?

3. In what ways do you guard your heart? Why is guarding your heart important?

4. Read Romans 12:14-21. Summarize this passage.

5. How can you apply this passage of scripture to your situation?

CHAPTER ELEVEN

<u>Bound by Bitterness</u>

Gloria had grown despondent since she put David out. She managed to climb out of bed and go to work for the first two weeks after she had kicked him out, but she soon found that it took too much energy to do anything more than get out of the bed to go to the bathroom. Consequently, Gloria took a short-term leave of absence from work. For the past couple of months she did nothing but eat and sleep...

═══════════════════════

In her depressed state Gloria had become a hermit. She only left the house for one reason: to re-stock her pantry. Needless to say, Gloria's weight had skyrocketed over the past couple of months. The once 150 pound "brick house" had become a prime candidate for a heart attack, weighing in excess of 230 pounds. She did not care about anything other than nursing her broken heart with her self-prescribed medicine – food.

Gloria spent her waking hours watching the soap operas on television. When the daytime line-up went off, she would switch to the Soap Channel and watch re-runs of old soaps. She identified with the characters who loved their man, but who had been mistreated and dogged by them. She bitterly described herself as a woman scorned, these days.

It didn't take long for the whole "Kendra thing" to get around her church. Stacey was understandably furious and she didn't waste anytime telling the Pastor and anyone else who would listen about how David had been sleeping with her daughter. Thankfully, Kendra was of age. Otherwise, Stacey and the church would have made sure that David was jailed for messing with jail bate. In fact, that boy would have been under the jail!

Gloria received periodic phone calls from her church family. They were genuinely concerned about her. Everyone knew how much she had wanted to make her marriage work. However, she used her privacy manager and caller I.D. to avoid taking any of their calls. Instead, she just listened as they left their message, and whenever she got up to go to the bathroom, she would hit the delete button on her answering machine to erase *the message.*

The only call that she took, on occasion, was Stephanie's. Their friendship dated back to middle school. They had been through a lot together; and if anyone understood how Gloria was feeling right now, it was Stephanie.

"How are you doing, Honey?" Stephanie asked. She had called Gloria almost everyday since she put David out. Stephanie was so worried about her. It was as if the Gloria that she had known all of her life had suddenly disappeared in an instant.

"I'm o.k." Gloria responded flatly.

"Have you been anywhere or talked to anyone this week?" Stephanie knew that Gloria hadn't moved from her bed, let alone the house, or answered any calls, but she thought that she would ask her anyway.

"Nope." Gloria's favorite soap, Twin Cities, was on so she was somewhat preoccupied.

"What about church?" Stephanie was trying not to show her exasperation with Gloria's attitude. For the last three months, Stephanie and Gloria had been having the same conversation over and over. Stephanie was beginning to get fed up with Gloria's prolonged pity party.

"What about it?" Gloria asked nonchalantly.

"Listen, you know that I love you. We have been friends for a long time, so I'm just going to take my chances and tell you how I really feel about the way that you have been acting. I know that you are hurting. I can only imagine how I would feel if I were in your shoes. I would, naturally, be devastated, BUT I couldn't remain there. You need to cut off that t.v. and get up off your butt. Go get your hair and your nails done. And more importantly, go back to church. I know that you are embarrassed, but you need a Word from God. He is the only one that can give you the comfort that you need right now. Put down those chips and pick up your Bible!" Stephanie was almost in tears. She was so afraid that her friend might not recover from this; she was afraid that Gloria would choose not to recover.

"You don't know the first thing about how I'm feeling. Your man has never cheated on you. As a matter of fact, you have it made. You have what everyone woman wants – a good man and a family. As far as church is concerned, you don't even attend one regularly. Do you even belong to a church?" Gloria asked lashing out at Stephanie.

Stephanie's first instinct was to take what Gloria said personally and become defensive, but something deep down inside of her stopped her. On the contrary, she suddenly felt giddy. She was overjoyed to finally get a passionate response out of Gloria even if it was negative. A negative response was better than the emotionless responses she had been getting for the last three months.

"You are absolutely right, Gloria. I don't know what it feels like to have been betrayed by my husband, but you can't stay embittered by what David did to you. I'm sure that from your perspective, it looks like I have everything that you have ever wanted. But aren't you *the one who told me that God is no respecter of persons? So if He did it for me, won't He do it for you? God has been waiting for you to submit to and trust in Him in ALL areas of your life. I'm sorry, but David was NOT the man that God had for you. David doesn't have nor does he want a relationship with God. But the man that God has for you, you have been perfectly fashioned for – your flesh of his flesh and bone of his bone."* Stephanie heard Gloria's quiet sobs as she paused to catch her breath.

"I'm here for you, Gloria. I will help you through this. I will pray with you and I will even go to church with you. Besides, it's not like I have a church home of my own, anyway." Stephanie said laughingly. She was trying to lighten the mood.

"That would be nice. My church will be happy to know that not only have I returned, but I brought another heathen to the Lord." Gloria said laughing now, too...

───────────

Stephanie, Keith and their children attended church with Gloria every Sunday. They enjoyed Gloria's church so much that they ended up joining. Church wasn't as awkward as Gloria thought it would be. For the most part, people treated her the same way as they always had. At first, there were a couple of people who appeared to be walking on eggshells around her, but things quickly went back to the way they once were. Her church family was just happy to have her back in church.

One Sunday, she mistakenly left her Bible in her car so she ran out to get it. As she walked back from her car through the church parking lot, David pulled up alongside of her. This was the last place that she expected to see him, so she was a bit startled by his sudden appearance.

"Glo', I'm happy that I caught you. I thought that I might have been too late. You know how you like to get to church early." He said smiling.

Gloria just looked at him with a blank face.

"Girl, you're looking good. You have really lost some weight. Listen Baby, I'm really sorry. I miss you. I mean, damn, don't you think that you put me through enough. I want you back." He said as smooth as ever.

"David, I'm not interested. I will never forgive you for what you did to me. The affair was just the icing on the cake. You mistreated me from the start of our marriage.

I want a man who will love me for me – not my dress size. Most importantly, I want a man who loves Jesus; a man who lives a committed life to the Word of God. Clearly, you're not that man."

"Here you go judging me again. Is that what your church friends told you, but you are supposed to be so holy, right? Then, what happened to forgiveness? Aren't you Christians supposed to "turn the other cheek?" He said accusingly.

"Yes, we are and I am still praying for God to help me to forgive you." With that said, and without looking back, Gloria turned around and headed back toward the church.

Overcoming Bitterness

We can all say that we have either been in a position where we were left feeling bitter because of a relationship, or that we know of at least one person who was bitter as a result of a relationship that ended badly. Many of us can easily identify with Gloria. You feel like you have given all that you have, only to be disappointed and taken advantage of in the end.

You can certainly see how that could leave one feeling a bit put out and disgusted. It's during these times that the Bible tells us to call on the Lord.

> Before they call I will answer;
> while they are still speaking I
> will hear (Isaiah 65:24).

> Let us then approach the
> throne of grace with confidence,
> so that we may receive mercy
> and find grace to help us in our
> time of need (Hebrews 4:16).

> Come near to God and he will
> come near to you...Humble
> yourselves before the Lord,
> and he will lift you up (James
> 4:8-10).

God is constantly watching over us. He never

sleeps nor slumbers and He is concerned with the things that concern us. More than our earthly fathers, God loves us and wants to protect us. When we stumble and fall He is there to pick us up. When we make bad choices, He is there to lovingly point us in the right direction. Our heavenly father patiently and tenderly comforts us through the growing pains of life.

---

*W*hen we allow
bitterness to take root
in our spirit, it limits
God's ability to use us.

Bitterness, like anger, binds you up by focusing all of your attention and energy on the situation. Consequently, you become so blinded and distracted by your circumstances that you are unable to see, appreciate, and learn from that which God is doing *through* your circumstances. The devil can't stop God from blessing you. Rather, his tactic is to have you so bound that you miss what God has for you.

When we allow bitterness to take root in our spirit, it limits God's ability to use us. Instead of being the light of the world and reflecting God's glory, we reflect the darkness from which bitterness and hate are born.

> Let all bitterness and
> indignation *and* wrath
> (passion, rage, and bad
> temper) and resentment (anger,
> animosity) and quarreling
> (brawling, clamor, contention)
> and slander (evil-speaking,
> abusive, blasphemous
> language) be banished from
> you, with all malice (spite, ill
> will, or baseness of any kind)
> Ephesians 4:31, AMP.

Change the Way you Think

Make a concerted effort to look for the positive. Sin is conceived in our minds. If we think about something long enough we will eventually act on that thought. If you think about how someone has mistreated you, naturally, you will become angry and ill feelings will result from that anger. Defeat the devil by changing the way you think!

> For the rest, brethren, whatever
> is true, whatever is worthy of
> reverence *and* is honorable
> *and* seemly, whatever is just,
> whatever is pure, whatever is
> lovely *and* lovable, whatever is
> kind *and* winsome *and* gracious,
> if there is any virtue *and*

> excellence, if there is anything
> worthy of praise, think on *and*
> weigh *and* take into account
> these things [fix your minds on
> them] (Philippians 4:8, AMP).

Also, read the Book of Ruth. If ever there were two women with a right to be bitter, it was them. After the death of her husband and two sons, Naomi was left to return to Judah and fend for herself. Naomi was very bitter about the death of her husband and sons and attributed her circumstances to God's discipline (1:13).

Naomi pleaded for both of her daughters-in-law to return home. Orpah returned to her homeland, but Ruth refused.

> But Ruth replied, "Don't urge
> me to leave you or to turn back
> from you. Where you go I will
> go, and where you stay I will
> stay. Your people will be my
> people and your God my God
> (1:16).

Now, honestly speaking, how many of us would have reacted that way? Think about it... you left your family, friends, home, and gods to marry your husband. He dies, and you're left with nothing. You can't even remarry because his only brother is dead, too. No one else can ensure that you will be taken care of. Your mother-in-law gives you the go ahead to cut your losses and run and you say, no? How many of us would have allowed the bitter seed to root and grow in our hearts because of these seemingly dire circumstances?

Because of Ruth's loyalty to Naomi and God, and because of her determination not to allow Naomi to become paralyzed by her bitterness or to become embittered herself, she met and married Boaz. She was rewarded richly - she is the mother of Obed and the great-grandmother of David, thus, making her an ancestor of Jesus (Matthew 1:5)! The Book of Ruth is just one example of women in the Bible whose perspective and belief in God enabled them to overcome their circumstances.

REFLECTION QUESTIONS

1. How can one be bound by bitterness?

2. What are the consequences of allowing bitterness to take root in your spirit?

3. How can you defeat the devil by changing the way that you think?

4. Read Philippians 4:8. How can you apply these verses of scripture to help you change the way that you think?

5. What can we learn from Ruth and how she handled seemingly dire circumstances?

CHAPTER TWELVE

Let the Captive Free!

Veronica could not forgive herself. She could not get past all of the hurt and pain that she had allowed Mike to cause her. He was the only man she had ever trusted and she gave him everything. He, on the other hand, had abused her trust and her faith...

═══════════════════════════════

God had really been keeping and providing for Veronica since that faithful day that she took her children and fled in the middle of the night. She was so scared. Mike told her a thousand times that he would kill her if she ever tried to leave him. She became paranoid as she constantly looked over her shoulders wondering when Mike would appear.

Through it all, Lori had been wonderful! She allowed Veronica and her kids to stay with her until Veronica could safely get on her feet. During the six weeks that Veronica and her kids stayed with her, Lori helped Veronica to get a new cell phone with a new number, find a new job, and secure a safe place for Veronica and her children to live. Lori helped Veronica enroll her children in new schools and daycare.

Initially, Veronica was a mess. She kept questioning whether or not she had made the right choice by leaving Mike. How in the world would she support herself and three kids? Mike had always made sure that their every need was met. Thank God for Lori, who shared God's word with her and encouraged her to look to God for support.

Don't worry, Veronica. God is with you. The Bible says that if God be for you, then who can be against you? Everything is going to work out. Just trust Him and He will order your steps. Remember, with Christ, all things are possible!" Lori was always there with encouraging words when Veronica felt like giving up.

"I know. I try to remind myself of all the things that God has already done for me and my kids, but, sometimes, I still get discouraged." Veronica said solemnly.

God blessed Veronica with a job at the Faith Temple Church as an Assistant Financial Officer. Veronica was very happy to get a job that was in line with the skills that she had gained as an Office Manager. She aspired to become a financial planner and go on to receive her series seven license so that she could help low-income people invest and yield a return on their money.

In addition, the church was a "safe place." She and Lori had met with their pastor to discuss Veronica's situation, and he assured her that she would be safe there.

"Veronica, thank you for trusting me enough to share your circumstances with me. Don't worry; we are a family. You will not be going through this alone. We will be praying you through this and helping you in any way that we can." Pastor Clark said.

"Thank you, Pastor Clark. Lori has helped me immensely. I don't know where my kids and me would be, right now, without her help. I feel like I have lost everything and starting over seems near to impossible." Veronica confessed.

"Veronica, we all go through trying times, but we must look to God and trust that He will work everything out for our good. Psalm 28:6-8 says, 'Praise be to the Lord, for he has heard my cry for mercy. The Lord is my strength and my shield; my heart trusts in him, and I am helped…' When you feel discouraged, meditate on that scripture."

"I will. I guess that I just get anxious when I think about what lies ahead."

"You're safe here. I have assigned Brother Baxter to watch over you while you are here at the church. From what I understand, Pastor Lori has obtained you a three-bedroom apartment at Towers Point, which is a secured high-rise. In addition, she has notified the Towers Point security office about your situation and supplied them with a copy of your protection order."

Yes, Pastor. They have assured me that the building and the underground-parking garage are secure. They have monitoring cameras on every floor and they are monitored 24 hours a day." Lori responded.

Veronica felt relieved and loved. No one else had ever taken such good care of her without getting or wanting something in return. Mike's love had come at a high price and was deficient at best. She never expected that her church would provide for her to make a fresh start.

While Veronica was trying to make a go at a new life, her kids were struggling to let go of their old one. Little Mike began rebelling and Madison started wetting the bed. Veronica tried to explain to them that mommy and daddy lived in separate houses without getting into the details.

"Just tell us the truth, mom. We left because Dad is a jerk. He beat you up!" Little Mike said. He was so angry. He had been through so much the last couple of months – he had to leave his home, school, and friends. He hated his new school and Veronica knew that he missed his father terribly.

"Watch your mouth, Mike. I don't ever want to hear you talk about your father in that manner again. Do you understand me? Mommy and Daddy had a disagreement and we can't live together anymore, but he is still your father." Veronica said sternly. It broke her heart to see her baby so angry. Truthfully, she found it difficult not to be angry herself.

"Yes, ma'am."

So much had changed for them. Veronica had to return her Lexus truck because she couldn't afford the lease payments and their new apartment didn't have half of the luxuries of their old house. Needless to say, she wasn't getting any help from Mike because he had no idea where she or the kids were. She knew that this was hard on he kids because they didn't really understand what was going on.

After she put the kids to bed at night, she would lay in her bed and cry herself to sleep. There were times when she felt so lonely and miserable that she contemplated ending it all. As quickly as the thought entered her mind, it was replaced with thoughts of her children. She reminded herself that she had to stay strong for them. Then she would pull out her Bible and read the Psalms until she fell asleep.

One day when she was out grocery shopping, she ran into Miss Nadine from the bank.

"How you doing, baby? Me and Ms. Jones have been so worried about you. You just up and quit, and we didn't know what was going on." Miss Nadine was so happy to see Veronica.

"I'm fine, Miss Nadine. I just found a better opportunity." Veronica was very guarded. She was careful not to reveal too much. The last thing that she needed was Miss Nadine all up in her business.

As if on queue, Miss Nadine said, "I'm not trying to

be all up in your business, but Mike came up to the bank looking for you. He asked us if we had seen you around. He said that you took the kids and left."

"Mike and I aren't together anymore, but I really don't want to talk about it."

"I understand. You know that I always thought that you could do better. Anyway, him and Tammy deserve each other."

"What?" Veronica started feeling weak as if she might faint at any moment.

"I'm sorry, I thought that's why you left him because you found out that he was cheating on you with Tammy." Miss Nadine was embarrassed. She truly thought that's why they had broken up, and now she wanted to kick herself for opening up her big mouth. " Baby, I told you that boy wasn't good for nothing. He's been gallivanting all around town with that girl. You know that she was always jealous of you. She couldn't wait to tell us how she had your man."

"It really doesn't matter anymore. We're not together so he's free to be with whomever he chooses." Veronica was surprised at how disinterested she sounded; all the while, on the inside, she felt like bolting to the bathroom so that she could throw-up.

Tears streamed down Veronica's face as she drove home from the grocery store. She felt so stupid! All this time she had been missing him, and he had already moved on to another woman. Veronica was deeply hurt. All of the pain that she felt quickly turned into hate.

"I hate him. I will never forgive him for what he has

done to me!" She screamed between her tears.

"That's exactly what I get for staying with him. I knew what it was from the beginning of our relationship, but I was too naive to demand more. I was so afraid of losing him that I let anything go. Then, I was too dumb to leave him once I realized that he would never be capable of loving me the way that a man should love a woman. I don't have anyone to blame, but myself. People treat you the way you allow yourself to be treated. How could he value me when I didn't even value myself?" She thought as she pulled into her parking garage. She parked her car, laid her head on her steering wheel and continued to cry.

Thankfully, the kids were at aftercare so she had some time to get herself together before she went to pick them up.

True Forgiveness

The New Webster's Dictionary and Roget's Thesaurus defines Forgive as, "To pardon; To remit; To overlook." True forgiveness requires dying to self. In order to forgive others we must first die to our own natural desires (being right, vindication, retribution, etc.) so that we can have the necessary compassion to excuse the offender despite their slights, shortcomings, and errors. As Christians, we are commanded to forgive others as God forgives us.

"For if you forgive men when
they sin against you, your

heavenly Father will also forgive you. But if you don't forgive men their sins, your Father will not forgive your sins (Matthew 6:14-15)."

"And when you stand praying, if you hold anything against anyone, forgive him, so that your Father in heaven may forgive you your sins (Mark 11:25)."

"Do not judge, and you will not be judged. Do not condemn, and you will not be condemned. Forgive, and you will be forgiven (Luke 6:37)."

God's Command to Forgive

When we are unwilling to forgive those who have transgressed against us then God will not forgive us. Our hardened heart, which causes us to sin due to disobedience, imprisons us and we become susceptible to God's wrath. For these reasons, it is imperative for us to learn how and be willing to forgive our brothers and sisters.

"Then the master called the servant in. 'You wicked

servant,' he said, 'I canceled all that debt of yours because you begged me to. Shouldn't you have had mercy on your fellow servant just as I had on you?' In anger his master turned him over to the jailers to be tortured, until he should pay back all that he owed. "This is how my heavenly Father will treat each of you unless you forgive your brother from your heart. (Matthew 18:32-35)."

God's forgiveness of us requires that we forgive others because grace brings responsibility and obligation. Jesus gave no limits on the extent that we are to forgive. Forgiveness shows that we are true followers of Christ by exemplifying that which God has given us through salvation. When we forgive then God can and will use us to be a blessing unto that person.

Take Joseph for example. His ten older brothers hated him because he was his father's favorite son (37:31) and because Joseph had dreams that he interpreted to his brothers in an egotistical way. Joseph was arrogant so it's not hard to imagine why they despised him enough to kill him (37:4). So one day when Jacob sent Joseph out to search for his brothers, they took their opportunity to try to kill him. At his brother Rueben's objections, they decided not to kill him, but instead to sell him to slavery.

Joseph was enslaved and then sent to prison. While in prison, Joseph interpreted the dreams of the Pharaoh's butler. When the Pharaoh started having dreams that no one else could interpret, the butler remembered Joseph. After Joseph interpreted the Pharaoh's dreams, he was appointed food commissioner. He was called Zapenath-Paneah, which means "revealer of secrets."

Many years later when the famine struck, Joseph's brothers had to come to Egypt to buy grain. When they met Joseph they didn't recognize him, but he recognized them. Although Joseph tested his brothers to see if they had changed, he didn't take revenge against them. Joseph forgave them. God's grace was evident in the way that Joseph dealt with his family. He realized that his suffering was an instrument of God's will that had preserved his family.

Forgiveness is necessary. God forgives us over and over for the things that we do that grieve Him. If we are to be used like Joseph, as an instrument of God's will, then we first have to forgive ourselves and then we have to release the person who hurt us. I'm not advocating that you should put yourself back into the same situation, but rather that you should forgive the person who abused you and pray for their deliverance.

REFLECTION QUESTIONS

1. In what ways do you have to die to self in order to offer someone forgiveness?

2. What does the Bible say will happen to us if we don't forgive?

3. Read Matthew 18:32-35. Summarize these verses in your own words.

4. How does "forgiveness" show the world that we are true followers of Christ?

5. How was Joseph used as an instrument of God's will? How can you be used as an instrument of God's will?

PART V

THE PATH TO PEACE

*You will guard him and keep him in perfect
and constant peace whose mind [both its
inclination and its character] is stayed on
You, because he commits himself to You, leans
on You, and hopes confidently in You.*
Isaiah 26:3 (AMP)

CHAPTER THIRTEEN

Trusting God

Things had been going really well for Veronica and her kids. Little Mike was adjusting to his new school and neighborhood. He had made a lot of new friends. Veronica was happy that he had some boys his age to play with. Madison stopped wetting the bed, too. Veronica and her children were receiving counseling from one of the members in the church who is a behavioral psychologist. Pastor Clark referred Veronica to Dr. Peters because he thought that Dr. Peters would be able to help them adjust to their new life...

—————————————————

"You wanted to see me, Pastor?" Veronica said as

she walked into his office.

"Yes, Veronica. I wanted to talk to you about the problems that Little Mike and Madison have been experiencing. I think that it would be best if you and the kids sought counseling from a behavioral psychologist. This would enable each of you to get some things out in the open so that they can be dealt with in the best manner. Despite your best efforts, it is likely that the kids may have witnessed some of the domestic violence and the result of that traumatic experience has now manifested itself in behavioral issues."

"Mike always made the kids go to their rooms, but our house was small and our bedroom was right next to theirs. So I'm sure that, if nothing else, there were times they may have heard us."

"With your permission, I would like to approach one of the sisters in the church who is a behavioral psychologist and runs her own private practice. She is very discreet and professional; she has counseled a number of families here at the church. If you are interested, I will personally make the arrangements and take care of any costs associated with the counseling."

Veronica didn't now what to say. She had wanted to go to counseling, but she didn't have the money. Her Pastor's thoughtfulness and generosity moved her.

"Thank you, Pastor. Of course you have my permission. I can't begin to tell you how much this means to my family and to me. Bless you!" Veronica couldn't wait to attend the first session; she had been so concerned about how her children had been affected by *all of this.*

Veronica was surprised by all that she learned during counseling. Not only had the children heard her screams, but they would all hide together in Little Mike's room as they sought comfort from one another. The violence terrified them. They thought that their father was going to kill their mother. Sometimes, when things got really bad, Little Mike would watch from his doorway.

All this time, she thought that little Mike was acting out because he missed his father, when in actuality Little Mike was acting out because he was torn between loving his father and hating his father. He hated his father for beating his mother, but he loved him because he knew that's what he was supposed to do. Little Mike felt guilty because he didn't like or respect his father.

Hearing her children talk about how scared they were almost killed Veronica. It took everything in her not to totally break down during their sessions. With the help of Dr. Peters, she assured the children that they were all safe now. She promised them that she would never place them in that kind of environment again. Together, she and her kids made great strides through counseling.

Things were going really well for her with regards to her job, too. With the knowledge that she gained from her employment at the bank, she was able to streamline the church's deposit process. In addition, she decided to go back to school and pursue a degree in finance.

Veronica was done playing the "victim." At last, she had gotten herself together. Her kids were settled, secure, and happy. She had come to a place where she knew the fullness of the joy of the Lord. She was tired of playing the "victim" and she wasn't going to play that role anymore! In the name of Jesus she was taking her life back, giving it over to God and trusting Him to be the Head – the author and finisher of her faith.

She had finally decided to go after Mike for child support. He had not made any attempt to see her or the children and she was fine with that. She believed God would provide for them and He had been faithful. She knew, however, that fear was not of God and that she would eventually have to face her demons in order to have victory in those areas of her life.

With that in mind, she filed for child support. On the day of her court date, she walked into the courtroom with her head held high. She didn't know what to expect; she didn't know if Mike would show up or not. But she prayed and knew that whatever happened, God was in complete control.

Mike did show up that day. Dressed in his usual – blue jeans, white T-shirt, and Timberland boots. Not only did he look the same, he behaved the same. He was just as cocky as ever.

When the case was settled, Veronica felt euphoric. She had courage to stand up to her Goliath and, like David, she had defeated him. As she exited the courtroom, Mike was there waiting for her.

"Veronica, can I talk to you for a minute?" He tried to look as menacing as possible. This was the same look that he would give her when he was displeased with her.

She turned around to face him as he walked over to her.

"So, you finally came crawling out of hiding. You think it's okay to show your face now? Oh, you think I'm not going to make good on my word? Didn't I tell you what would happen if you ever tried to leave me?"

"You know what? You don't scare me anymore. Nothing scares me. You might hunt me down, you can threaten to kill me, and you may be successful. You can kill the body, but you can't kill my soul. My soul belongs to God. I will not walk in fear of you, of any situation, or of anyone else because I know the God that I serve. I know that His angels encamp about me, that He keeps me from hurt, harm and danger. The Bible says that He hides me under his wing. Do what you have to do, just know that the Bible says, "Touch not mine anointed." When you mess with me, then you have to deal with my heavenly Father. I'm the daughter of the Most High God."

Mike was dumfounded. He stood there looking stupid. He didn't know what to say. He had never seen this side of Veronica.

"Now, you be blessed, Mike." Veronica turned around and walked away. Never in her life had she felt so free! She finally knew what it meant to be free in the Lord – free from anxiety, worry, and fear. She understood that God is the ultimate protector. All the things that she was looking for in man she would only find in her Lord and Savior. God had given her everything that she ever needed and the desires of her heart, too! She walked out of the courthouse excited about going to the next level in

God, embracing the call on her life.

God is Always in Control

Trusting God enables us to place each concern, all worry, and every problem into His hands. In exchange, God fills us with peace that surpasses all understanding.

> You will keep in perfect peace him whose mind is steadfast, because he trusts in you. Trust in the Lord forever, for the Lord, the Lord, is the Rock eternal (Isaiah 26:3-4).

> If you do this, you will experience God's peace, which is far more wonderful than the human mind can understand. His peace will guard your hearts and minds as you live in Christ Jesus (Philippians 4:7, NLT).

No matter what the outward appearance, circumstances, or details of your situation, God is in full control. Nothing goes unnoticed by God. In fact, nothing happens to us that God has not already sanctioned. With that in mind, what does it profit us to continue to try to "fix", orchestrate, plan, or control our lives?

> But when the Holy Spirit
> controls our lives, he will
> produce this kind of fruit in
> us:...peace...(Galatians 5:22,
> NLT).

> The mind of sinful man is
> death, but the mind controlled
> by the Spirit is life and peace
> (Romans 8:6).

Mary – an Example of Faith

I'm sure that Mary planned to live a "normal" life. She was betrothed to Joseph and she looked forward to sharing a quiet existence with him. Like every woman, she probably wanted children and envisioned she and Joseph rearing them as they grew old together. However, that all changed when the angel, Gabriel, appeared to her and announced that she would give birth to the Messiah.

> But the angel said to her, "Do
> not be afraid, Mary, you have
> found favor with God. You will
> be with child and give birth
> to a son, and you are to give
> him the name Jesus. He will
> be great and will be called the

> Son of the Most High...the Holy
> Spirit will come upon you, and
> the power of the Most High will
> overshadow you. So the holy
> one to be born will be called
> the Son of God...For nothing
> is impossible with God (Luke
> 1:30-37).

Imagine how perplexing this must have been for Mary. She was a virgin and yet she was going to have a baby without the benefit of having known a husband intimately. She believed what Gabriel told her and she trusted God. Mary accepted her role without question; she is a model of faith. She trusted God even though she did not understand everything. Mary understood what we all need to understand – God keeps His promises regardless of how difficult the circumstances may seem.

> "I am the Lord's servant," Mary
> answered. "May it be to me
> as you have said." Then the
> angel left her (Luke 1:38).

Hope

Trusting God gives us hope. The New Webster's Dictionary and Roget's Thesaurus define hope as:

> *n.* A desire of some good,
> accompanied by the belief

that is attainable; trust; one
in whom trust or confidence is
placed; the object of hope.

Hope is confident expectancy. Hope is not derived from our wishes or desires, but is given to us by God. God is the believer's hope. Hope is not wishful thinking, but firm assurance that despite what we see in the natural, God is working in the supernatural.

May the God of hope fill you
with all joy and peace as you
trust in him, so that you may
overflow with hope by the power
of the Holy Spirit (Romans
15:13).

1. What does God promise to give those who trust in Him?

2. What does it profit you to continue to try to control your life?

3. How is Mary an example of faith?

4. How can you learn from Mary and increase your faith?

5. What is hope?

CHAPTER FOURTEEN

Love Yourself

Gloria was back to her old self. She had filed for divorce from David on the grounds of adultery. She had put the past and all of its pain behind her. She had gone back to work and received a promotion. She was truly happy now because things seem to have come full circle.

She was back working at the church and was diligently trying to lose the weight that she had gained. For the first time in her life, she was determined to take care of her temple, not for vain reasons, but because she wanted to honor the Lord. Her body is the temple of the Holy Spirit and she wanted to represent God by both her inner spirit and outer man.

Gloria spent most of her free time studying God's Word. She knew that if she were able to discipline herself with regard to her eating habits, then she would be able to discipline herself in other areas of her life. In hindsight, she was thankful that she had gone through all that she had with David. She was much more spiritually mature. Had she been as disciplined before, perhaps she would not have made the same bad choices.

Gloria learned, slowly, to forgive David. God had softened her heart. She was tired of being angry and hating David. Hating him was draining her and turning her into a person that she didn't know or like. Instead of looking at the glass as half full, as she used to before David, she saw it as half-empty. She became cynical, dry, and unmoved by anything.

Gloria put walls up around her heart that were so thick that she was no longer confident about any of her feelings. She knew then that something had to give for fear that she would never be able to identify with her feelings again. She had ministered to women like that before who, because of their situations, had grown cold and callused.

She definitely was not going to continue to allow David to have that kind of power over her. More importantly, she wanted to please God. She knew that God was not pleased with her attitude or her thoughts. Although she set her mind to forgive David, it wasn't that easy. In her heart and her Spirit, she understood that forgiving David was going to have to be something that

God gave her the strength and the grace to do.

Gloria consecrated herself to the Lord and went on a twenty-one day fast. During this time, she abstained from food and studied her Bible. She did not talk on the phone nor did she watch television. She communed with God and allowed Him to purge her of every ill feeling and unholy thought that she had concerning David.

She met God in her guestroom –turned prayer room each and every day. As she praised and worshipped God, she felt the hate begin to slip away until it was no longer there. God had replaced it with compassion and mercy. Instead of talking about David, she prayed for him. Every time she mentioned his name, she would ask God to bless and keep him. She also prayed (this time with pure, unselfish motives) for his salvation.

It was during her fast that she rededicated her life to God. She repented for turning away from God and compromising her walk to be unequally yoked with David. She also repented for allowing herself to get out of shape both physically and spiritually. She promised herself and God that she would not get distracted again – she would keep her eyes on the Lord and obey his commands.

Stephanie and her family had been very supportive of Gloria. They had grown incredibly close. "Auntie Glo", as Stephanie's kids affectionately called her, was a honorary member of their family. Like Gloria, Stephanie had come into her own, spiritually. She had matured greatly. She had a voracious hunger and thirst for God's Word. Stephanie was Gloria's iron. The Bible says that iron sharpens iron and that's what Stephanie did for

Gloria. She held her accountable for and encouraged her with the Word of God.

The two women became study and workout buddies. They attend a spinning class on Mondays and do Yoga on Wednesdays. Gloria was so focused on her workout that she didn't notice that Robert, their spinning instructor, was flirting with her.

"I wish that I could get some attention in the class. Robert's so focused on you that I could fall off my bike and he wouldn't notice." Stephanie teased.

"Whatever! He encourages everybody in the class." Gloria said, dismissing Stephanie.

"Why is it that you just can't accept that a man might be attracted to you?" Stephanie asked. She thought that Gloria's self-confidence had improved since she lost weight.

"Stephanie, I'm still 30 pounds over weight. It's not like I stop traffic when I walk down the street."

"The devil is a liar! Stop judging yourself by the world's standards. Doesn't the Bible say that you are fearfully and wonderfully created? God made you in His image and you are beautiful. The man that God sends looking for you will be first attracted to your spirit, then your body. You need to learn how to love yourself. No one will love you unless you love yourself."

As much as Gloria hated to admit it, Stephanie made a lot of sense. In truth, she didn't love herself but that was about to change. When she went home that night, she opened her Bible to study about God's love. Sometime around 3:00 a.m. that morning, she came to discern who she was in God. The knowledge of God's love helped her to, at last, accept and love herself.

Two weeks later, Robert asked Gloria out for coffee. She was extremely nervous, but she accepted his invitation. They learned a great deal about each other over coffee. It didn't take long for them to become comfortable with one another as they found out that they had much in common. Beginning with the fact that they were both Christians!

Not wanting to make the same mistake twice, Gloria took her time with this relationship. She didn't want to presume or rush into anything. They just enjoyed each other's company. From time to time they visited each other's churches. They even started meeting with Stephanie and Keith to do Bible study together.

They had been together for about six months, yet Keith never pressured Gloria into anything. They were both living celibate lives devoted, first, to the Lord. Because they were both very serious about their walk, they supported each other in the pursuit to "press towards the mark." Neither one wanted to do anything to destroy their testimony or offend God.

God blessed them with a relationship that was built on Him. Unlike her relationship with David, Gloria was not clouded by her desires or by the complications that result from a sinful sexual relationship. Together, they were focused on the Lord. Their relationship was beautiful because it was Christ centered. They agreed that when the time was right, they would fast to get direction from God as to whether or not they should take their relationship to the next level. Whatever the direction, this time Gloria was confident that God would work everything out for her good!

Created in His Image

Before you can go any further, you must learn to love yourself. If you can't love yourself, then you will not be able to love anyone else. Free yourself from guilt and self-hatred. Regardless of your age, weight, sex, height, skin color, ethnicity, education, profession, etc., you are fearfully and wonderfully created (Psalm 139:14) and God intends to fulfill his purpose for you (Psalm 138:8).

Stand in front of a mirror and look at yourself. Really look at yourself. God sent Jesus, the perfect sacrifice to die for the person reflected in the mirror. That's how much God loves you! Bear in mind that God created you in His own image (Genesis 1:27) so if you hate yourself, then you hate God. The world's standards do not matter. The only perception that matters is God. Unlike the world, God is not concerned with your appearance. He is concerned with your heart.

> But the Lord said to Samuel, "Do not consider his appearance or his height, for I have rejected him. The Lord does not look at the things man looks at. Man looks at the outward appearance, but the Lord looks at the heart (1 Samuel 16:7)."

As water reflects a face, so a
man's heart reflects the man
(Proverbs 27:19).

He said to them, "You are the
ones who justify yourselves
in the eyes of men, but God
knows your hearts. What is
highly valued among men is
detestable in God's sight (Luke
16:15)."

Mistakes: Opportunities for Growth

We all make mistakes. The test is in how we
respond to those mistakes. The difference between a
Christian and an unsaved individual is that we have to
get back up. We can't let life's circumstances get us to
the point where we don't want to or think that we can't
make it. God created us to be victorious in the Name of
Jesus! The Bible says that, " No, in all these things we
are more than conquerors through him who loved us
(Romans 8:37)." The trials and tribulations of life make
us more than conquerors by forcing us to depend even
more on God.

Not only so, but we also rejoice
in our sufferings, because we
know that suffering produces
perseverance; perseverance,
character; and character, hope.

> And hope does not disappoint
> us, because God has poured
> out his love into our hearts
> by the Holy Spirit, who he has
> given us (Romans 5:3-5).

Stop beating yourself for the bad choices that you've made, by all means thank God for life's ups and downs and, most of all, for the lessons learned along the way. Rejoice in your situation because the Lord foreknew you and, in His infinite wisdom, knew that you would be where you are at this very moment in time.

As Christians, we know that nothing happens by chance. We serve a mighty God who doesn't make mistakes. God gives us free will and allows us to make our own decisions. Though we may not always make the right choice, "We are assured *and* know that [God being a partner in their labor] all things work together *and* are [fitting into a plan] for good to *and* for those who love God and are called according to [His] design *and* purpose (Romans 8:28 AMP).

Though you have suffered hardship, don't be disheartened. God is not through with you yet! God is using these experiences to perfect you and mature you (James 1:2-4). This is but your Sea of Galilee and God is doing great things in and through you, but you have to hold on and trust God. Remember that He can say to the winds "Quiet! Be still!" and they will cease (Mark 4:39). Bonds will be broken and souls will be delivered through your testimony when you get to the other side

(Mark 4:35).

So buckle down and get rooted and grounded in God's Word. Have faith and encourage yourself because this valley experience is designed to take you to another level in God. The Bible says:

> Moreover [let us also be full of joy now!] let us exalt *and* triumph in our troubles *and* rejoice in our sufferings, knowing that pressure *and* affliction *and* hardship produce patience *and* unswerving endurance. And endurance (fortitude) develops maturity of character (approved faith and tried integrity). And character [of this sort] produces [the habit of] joyful and confident hope of eternal salvation. Such hope never disappoints *or* deludes *or* shames us, for God's love has been poured out in our hearts through the Holy Spirit Who has been given to us (Romans 5:3-5 AMP).

REFLECTION QUESTIONS

1. What parts of yourself do you find "unlovable?" What does Psalm 139:14 say about those parts?

2. How have you let the trials and tribulations of life force you to depend more on God?

3. How has God used your "mistakes" for your good?

4. What experience is God using, currently, to perfect and mature you?

CHAPTER FIFTEEN

<u>Unshakable Joy</u>

"It's a new season; it's a new day. Fresh anointing is flowing my way. It's a season of power and prosperity. It's a new season coming to me...All that was stolen is returned to you a hundred fold. Tried in the fire but you're coming out gold. Cling to His hand; yes, to every promise take a hold. It's a new season!" Kim sang along with her Martha Munizzi C.D. that she had blasting in her car stereo.

Today was the court hearing for her uncontested divorce. Her divorce was final and she was at last, legally, free from Conrad. In reality, she had long since divorced him in her heart; the divorce decree was just a formality. She was extremely happy to end that chapter of her life.

════════════════════════════════

Kim had come to a place in her life where she had the joy of the Lord. It bubbled up out of her. As of late, she was undaunted by what she heard Conrad was saying or doing. Freely, she gave her feelings, pains, disappointments, and anger to the lord. God had given her discernment, and she knew that unless she resisted the enemy he would continue to try to use Conrad as a means to hold her back.

Kim resisted the devil at all costs because this battle meant the difference of spiritual life or death for her. Everyday, she made a conscience decision to live in the Name of Jesus. In turn, God had given her His joy – joy that is not based on circumstances. The devil didn't give it to her and he can't take it away.

Kim was still supporting Jordan, in the natural, alone. It didn't take long, however, for her to realize that her "manna" came from God. Everything that Kim needed, God provided. She was only working part-time, yet she always seemed to have all the money that she needed. Not only did God use her parents, Jean and Jackson, to bless her but the favor of the Lord rested on her.

Each month, she hit and exceeded the goals set for her at her job. She would bring home incentive checks that doubled her regular pay. God kept the devourer at bay and went before her to make her path straight. She had learned to trust God in everything – despite what the situation looked like in the natural.

This was a great encouragement to Jean. She always appreciated the fact that her daughter was strong, but she now understood that Kim's strength came from the Lord. As a result, Jean desired to go deeper in her relationship with the Lord.

"Kim, you have a good relationship with the Lord. He always answers your prayers."

"Mom, He'll answer yours, too. All you have to do is have faith, and He will answer your prayers. Praying is nothing more than having a conversation with God. Just remember that a conversation is two-sided. When you ask God something, you must wait and listen for His answer." Kim enjoyed talking to her mother about the Lord and the Bible. She was excited that God used the turmoil in her life to draw her mother closer to Him.

God had also been confirming Kim's women's ministry. About two years ago, God gave Kim a night vision. She dreamt that she and two other women were at a young girl's house trying to minister to her. The young girl was a member of Satan's army; Kim and the other women were trying to win her over for Christ. They almost had the young girl won over for Christ when, suddenly, her sister walked in and began yelling at her for allowing Kim to minister to her. Just then, Kim heard a noise; she looked out the window. Lined up and down the entire street were Satan and his army. Kim beckoned to the other two girls to follow her.

"It's just the three of us against an entire army; I

think that we should leave." Kim said to the others.

In the next instance, Kim was alone holding her daughter, Jordan. She stood face to face with Satan and his army. She noticed that the army consisted of only women and children. Satan called Kim out and, at first, she was terrified. But she felt the boldness of the Lord come upon her as she sat Jordan down while she and the devil did battle.

Kim defeated the devil with the Word of God. She continued to quote scripture, as Jesus did when He was in the desert being tempted, until the devil was defeated. When she looked at the army of women and children, some of the women were laughing at the devil while others looked amazed that she had actually beat the devil.

Then she woke up.

It was later confirmed, through interpretation and prophecy that God had given Kim the awesome responsibility of ministering to women. At first she thought that her ministry would involve counseling married women, however, she was concerned that God would not continue to use her due to her failed marriage. She grossly underestimated the Lord. In his infinite wisdom, for he knows our "story" before we know it, God intended to use Kim and her life experiences to minister to women whose spirits had been crippled and disfigured due to domestic violence and abuse.

When Kim left Zion Hill Baptist, God sent her to

Everlasting Church of God. She and Jordan enjoyed their new church immensely. There she found deliverance and healing in the preached Word of God. She was ecstatic that God immediately planted her in another ministry where she and Jordan would be loved, encouraged, and covered. More importantly, she knew that at Everlasting she would be rooted and grounded in the Word of God.

Not long after she joined, she met with the senior pastors, Charles and Barbara Thomas. She expressed her appreciation for their ministry and shared her testimony with them.

"Thank you for meeting with me Pastor Charles and Barbara. I just wanted to tell you how much your ministry and the work that the two of you are doing for the Lord has impacted my life. When I joined Everlasting Church of God, I had just filed for divorce. My ex husband is an associate pastor at my old church and he was psychologically and physically abusive. Although I knew that ending my marriage was the right thing to do, leaving Zion Hill was still very difficult for me." Kim confessed.

"Is your ex husband still the associate pastor at Zion Hill?" Pastor Charles asked.

"As far as I know. It is also my understanding that he accepts preaching engagements in various churches around the city." Kim replied.

"That's distressing. Christian marriages are supposed to be stronger due to faith in and adherence to God's Word. Did you seek help from the church?" Pastor Brenda said, concerned.

"Yes, we had counseling both inside and outside of the church. Ultimately I realized that you can pray and fast, but the abuser must have a desire to line up with the Word of God. God gave us all free will. He is a gentleman and will never force Himself on anyone; it's up to us to choose Him over the world."

"That's right." Pastors Charles and Barbara said in unison.

"You don't realize that marriage is a ministry when you're single; in your haste to get married, you discount your singleness. It is during our singleness that God prepares each mate for the ministry of marriage. It is when we get ahead of Him that we enter into the marriage ill-prepared." Kim continued.

"You are very mature and God is going to use you mightily. The very things that the devil attempted to kill within you are the very things that are going to catapult you to the next level in the kingdom" Pastor Charles said smiling.

"Bless you, Pastor. With that said, let me share the ministry that God gave to me with you. It's called D.O.C., an acronym for Daughters of Christ.

When you're sick and you need to be healed you go to the doctor. Who's the doctor of all doctors? God. D.O.C. is for women like me – not single (in the purest sense of the word) and not married.

D.O.C. gives women who are "stuck in the middle" an opportunity to fellowship, share their testimonies and get healing. Women who have been in abusive relationships and who have divorced their husbands, as an act of survival, don't have anywhere to go in the Church. We feel like outcasts because we don't "fit in" anywhere. How many times have you preached a sermon that encourages divorcees as compared to the times that you have preached on topics geared towards singles and/or married couples?

Women, stuck in the middle, are in need of encouragement, understanding, and empathy. Due to fear, poor judgement, and/or ridicule these women don't feel comfortable sharing their testimonies. I have met and have had the opportunity to minister to many women who feel displaced in the church because of their personal circumstances; some of these women even attend Everlasting Church of God. With your blessing, I would like to establish D.O.C. here at Everlasting and open it up to women all over the city. It is my prayer that this will, one day, become an International Ministry for Christian women." Kim shared.

"Sister Kim, you have just confirmed something that God gave me – well, gave to both of us. God placed this same idea on the Pastor's heart and my heart some time ago. He had been showing us women in our congregation who were spiritually broken and battered. We bless God for your obedience!" Pastor Brenda said as her eyes filled with tears.

━━━━━━━━━━━━━━━━━━

It's amazing how the Lord works when you are obedient. That meeting was prophetic in so many ways. In the first year, D.O.C. impacted over 500 women city wide.

By the third year, D.O.C. was a nationally recognized ministry with a newsletter that was subscribed to by over 30,000 women. An annual conference attended by more than 10,000 women. Like Jabez, Kim asked the Lord to increase her territory and He had. Kim was speaking and sharing her testimony at women's retreats, conferences, and churches worldwide.

The joy that she felt was immeasurable. Yes, she had been through a lot, but God had been with her through it all. She went into the fiery furnace but came out unscathed. In fact, she thanked God for the trials and tribulations because, without them, she wouldn't be the woman of God that she'd grown to be. When things became challenging, she always remembered what the Holy Spirit taught her – in the natural ,pressure bursts pipes but in the supernatural, it creates diamonds. She was God's diamond in the rough!

What is Joy?

Joy is a positive attitude caused by acquisition or expectation of good; delight; exultation. Joy which is different than mere happiness is not contingent on our circumstances. It is born out of the Holy Spirit. When we are obedient to God, then we have joy that is holy and pure.

> But when the Holy Spirit controls our lives, he will produce this kind of fruit in us:...joy...(Galatians 5:22,

NLT).

---

*A*s Christians, we can have joy in the midst of sorrow. Even at a time of great loss and grief we have joy because we know that the Lord is with us.

God-given Joy supersedes our present circumstances and focuses on the character of God. It enables us to delight in the Lord. God does not promise temporary happiness. On the contrary, the Bible warns us that we will have troubles, but God is faithful to reward all who believe in Him with everlasting joy.

> Then I will go to the altar of God,
> to God, my joy and my delight.
> I will praise you with the harp,
> O God my God (Psalm 43:4).

> "As the father has loved me, so have I loved you. Now remain in my love. If you obey my commands, you will remain in my love, just as I have obeyed my father's commands and

remain in his love. I have told you this so that my joy may be in you and that your joy may be complete (John 15:9-11)."

As Christians, we can have joy in the midst of sorrow. Even at a time of great loss and grief, we have joy because we know that the Lord is with us. When we are persecuted for Christ's sake, we should be glad because difficult circumstances help us to better understand what Christ went through in order to make us partners with him.

I know the Lord is always with me ...No wonder my heart is filled with joy...(Psalm 16:8-9, NLT).

Dear friends, do not be surprised at the painful trial you are suffering, as though something strange were happening to you. But rejoice that you participate in sufferings of Christ, so that you may be overjoyed when his glory is revealed (1 Peter 4:12-13).

How do I Keep God's Joy?
Taking control of your thoughts will help you keep

your joy when the devil comes to plant seeds of doubt and destruction. The devil loves nothing more than to be able to steal your joy. For this reason, we have to protect our joy. Guard your joy by having faith and trusting that God will do what He said He would do.

We also find joy in God's righteousness, His mercy, creation, Word, and His faithfulness. Most importantly, we find joy in our salvation. Hope in God's promise for eternal life brings us joy because we know that what we are presently going through, one day, will end.

> Restore to me the joy of your salvation and grant me a willing spirit, to sustain me (Psalm 51:12).

Praising and worshiping God for who He is and all that He has done for us reinforces and guarantees our joy. Just think about all that God has done for you. Does it bring tears to your eyes and joy overflowing out of your heart? Has God kept you when you didn't deserve to be kept? Has God provided for you time and time again even though you griped and complained that you don't have your heart's desires? If you have eternal life, use of your body and a sound mind, you should be leaping and shouting right now with the joy of the Lord!

---

*T*he devil meant to kill
you and when he couldn't
do that, he tried to maim
you for life.

We also need to press into the Lord during times of uncertainty in order to keep our joy. Habakkuk had to learn to press into the Lord and praise Him in the midst of death and destruction. The Babylonian armies were on a killing rampage and had already defeated Assyria and Egypt. God gave Habakkuk a vision that confirmed that Judah would be next. Habakkuk was shocked and distraught by the news that God intended to use the Babylonians as an instrument of judgement (2:4). Because of his great faith in God, in the midst of his indignation, Habakkuk was filled with joy and praised God (3:18).

In essence, hold onto God no matter what things are like now; just continue to hold onto God. The Bible tells us that God equips the called (Hebrew 13:21, 2 Timothy 3:17). This means that He has given you everything that you need to be victorious. Bad choices that you've made notwithstanding, God intends to use every one of your experiences for your good.

The devil meant to kill you and when he couldn't do that, he tried to maim you for life. The devil expected you to be so handicapped by the shame of the abuse that you would believe that you were not worthy to be used by God. He wanted you to feel worthless and tainted. But he underestimated you, Child of God! It is because of your life's "rough road" that you will be able to speak life to another woman's, otherwise, dead situation.

Do you realize that you are coming out of the valley? Thank God that you survived. There were times when you didn't think that you were going to make it, but by His grace and His mercy, you survived! He even kept you when you didn't *want* to make it. Now it's time for you to stand up and take your rightful place in the Kingdom.

Claim it! Confess it with your mouth and believe it in your heart – say, "I will survive in Jesus' Name!"

REFLECTION QUESTIONS

1. What is joy?

2. As a Christian, how do you have joy in sorrow?

3. How can controlling your thoughts enable you to keep your joy?

4. How do you guard your joy?

5. What can you do to reinforce and guarantee your joy?

Radmacher, Earl, Allen, Ron, House, H. Wayne. *Compact Bible Commentary*. Nashville, TN: Thomas Nelson, 2004.

Rupert, Dennis. *Biblical Fasting: What it is and how to do it.* new-life.net. 8 May 2005. <http://www.new-life.net/fasting.htm>.

Strong, James. *The New Strong's Exhaustive Concordance of the Bible*. Nashville, TN: Thomas Nelson, 1995.

TouchPoints. Wheaton, IL: Tyndale house, 1996.

Christian Fasting. AllAboutGod.com. 8 May 2005. <http://www.allaboutgod.com/christian-fasting.htm>.

Christian Fasting - What does the Bible Say? Gotquestions.org. 8 May 2005. <http://www.gotquestions.org/fasting.html>.

What is the Christian Answer to Domestic Violence? Gotquestions.org. 3 March 2005. <http://www.gotquestions.org/domestic-violence.html>.

Is Abuse an Acceptable Reason for Divorce? Gotquestions.org. 3 March 2005. <http://www.gotquestions.org/abuse-divorce.html>.

If you would like to correspond with Jenniifer in response to *I Will Survive In Jesus' Name!*, or to schedule speaking engagements, you can contact her at:

JENNIFER MITCHELL EARLEY
c/o APHESIS PUBLISHING COMPANY
P.O. Box 221366
BEACHWOOD, OH 44122

EMAIL: WWW.APHESISPUBLISHING.COM

Order Form

❧ Yes! I want_____ copies of *I Will Survive In Jesus' Name!* at $15.95 each plus $4 shipping and handling per book (Ohio Residents please add $1.28 sales tax per book). Canadian Orders must be accompanied by a postal money order in U.S. funds. Allow 15 days for delivery.

❧ My check or money order for $_____ is enclosed.

Name_____

Organization_____

Address_____

City/State/Zip_____

Phone_____

Email_____.

Mail to: Aphesis Publishing Company
P.O. Box 221366
Beachwood, OH 44122

Coming Soon...

FASTEN YOUR SEATBELT: THERE'S SOME BUMPS IN THE ROAD

NAVIGATING YOUR CHRISTIAN WALK

Learn how to:
- Handle **Potholes of Despair** and pay tithes and offerings at **Toll Booths.**
- How to go at the pace that God sets when, **Look Out, the Speed Limit Changed!**
- Pray during **Sudden Stops**
- Rely solely on God because **Warning, Radar Detectors are Illegal in this State!**
- Remember that God created you with a purpose and destiny, so you have been equipped for **Changing the Tires**